Don't Let Your Emotions Run Your Life For Teens

Dialectical Behavior Therapy Skills For Helping You Manage Mood Swings, Control Angry Outbursts & Get Along With Others

Sheri Van Dijk, MSW

16pt

Copyright Page from the Original Book

Publisher's Note

This publication is designed to provide accurate and authoritative information in regard to the subject matter covered. It is sold with the understanding that the publisher is not engaged in rendering psychological, financial, legal, or other professional services. If expert assistance or counseling is needed, the services of a competent professional should be sought.

INSTANT HELP, the Clock Logo, and NEW HARBINGER are trademarks of New Harbinger Publications, Inc.

Distributed in Canada by Raincoast Books

Copyright © 2021 by Sheri Van Dijk
Instant Help Books
An imprint of New Harbinger Publications, Inc.
5674 Shattuck Avenue
Oakland, CA 94609
www.newharbinger.com

Cover design by Amy Shoup

Acquired by Tesilya Hanauer

Edited by Brady Kahn

All Rights Reserved

Library of Congress Cataloging-in-Publication Data

Names: Van Dijk, Sheri, author.
Title: Don't let your emotions run your life for teens : dialectical behavior therapy skills for helping you manage mood swings, control angry outbursts, and get along with others / Sheri Van Dijk.
Other titles: Do not let your emotions run your life for teens
Description: Second Edition. | Oakland : New Harbinger Publications, 2021. | Revised edition of the author's Don't let your emotions run your life for teens, c2011. | Includes bibliographical references.
Identifiers: LCCN 2021005092
Subjects: LCSH: Emotions in adolescence--Juvenile literature. | Adolescent psychology--Juvenile literature. | Dialectical behavior therapy--Juvenile literature.
Classification: LCC BF724.3.E5 V36 2021 | DDC 155.5/124--dc23
LC record available at https://lccn.loc.gov/2021005092

TABLE OF CONTENTS

Praise for the first edition:	iv
Introduction	viii
CHAPTER ONE: Mindfulness: Learning Self-Awareness	1
CHAPTER TWO: What You Need to Know About Emotions	32
CHAPTER THREE: Taking Control of Out-of-Control Emotions	63
CHAPTER FOUR: Reducing Your Painful Emotions	101
CHAPTER FIVE: Surviving a Crisis Without Making It Worse	141
CHAPTER SIX: Improving Your Mood	161
CHAPTER SEVEN: Improving Your Relationships	183
CHAPTER EIGHT: Putting It All Together	216
Answers	227
Additional Reading	229
References	233
Back Cover Material	238

"Sheri Van Dijk has provided a delightful, must-read guide packed with important information for practitioners working with teens. Throughout, one can find practical, concrete, step-by step instructions that demystify the teenage emotional experience and offer practical tools. The numerous real-life vignettes validate the human experience and illustrate how to implement interventions to reduce painful emotions, which will resonate with clients and clinicians alike."

—**Ita Tobis, MSW, RSW,** director of campus programming at JACS Toronto

"*Don't Let Your Emotions Run Your Life for Teens* is a clear, concise, and helpful guide for teens. It offers tools to manage negative thoughts and feelings. Throughout this workbook you will find relatable exercises and techniques to help you regain control over your thoughts. Sheri Van Dijk has done it again! This workbook offers our teens the opportunity to practice their most needed skills in areas such as self-awareness, effective communication, and healthy relationships."

—**Stephen Cruickshank, CYC (Cert),** child and youth worker in acute outpatient services at Royal Victoria Regional Health Centre, and child youth counselor for child and adolescent inpatient mental health at Southlake Regional Health Centre

"With a compassionate approach of validation, challenge, and acceptance, Van Dijk has developed a workbook for teens dealing with intense emotions. It is filled with relevant, insightful, and clearly illustrated concepts. The ongoing thought-provoking yet gentle questioning ensures the reader's understanding. By including skill building exercises and activities that target thoughts, feelings, and behaviors, Van Dijk has created a wonderful, user-friendly, and concrete experience for teens."

—**Janice LeBlanc,** registered psychotherapist, registered art therapist, and certified trauma and resilience practitioner

"Sheri's new book teaches teens healthy ways of naming emotions, and the skills to move through distressing moments in their everyday experience. I love that the book is constructed in such a way that it can be used section by section, or one exercise at a time. The personal stories shared are very relevant to the current social environment experienced by youth, and the practice exercises are easy to follow."

—**Kinsey Lewis,** registered psychotherapist with more than twenty-five years' experience in community mental health with a special focus on transitional-age youth (16-24)

"Sheri Van Dijk is an expert in dialectical behavior therapy (DBT), and the second edition of *Don't Let Your Emotions Run Your Life for Teens* is another significant tool for helping teens through the emotional ups and downs of both average adolescence and more critical situations. Van Dijk teaches effective skills couched in relatable teen language and scenarios, so readers don't get lost or feel intimidated by professional jargon. Excellent resource!"

—**Lisa M. Schab, LCSW,** psychotherapist; and author of eighteen self-help books, including the teen journals, *Put Your Worries Here* and *Put Your Feelings Here*

"*Don't Let Your Emotions Run Your Life For Teens* has been my number one go-to resource book for guiding teens toward exploring with respect and curiosity their emotions, perceptions, and the value of learning how to "Walk the Middle Path." The DBT skills and worksheets are presented with exceptional clarity and relevance making the therapeutic work engaging and informative. A tremendous resource when navigating through the wonderful maze of our lives. Recommended for home, clinical, or personal use."

—**Mitchell E. Beube, MSW, RSW,** child, family, individual, and DBT group therapist

Praise for the first edition:

"*Don't Let Your Emotions Run Your Life for Teens* examines many areas that teenagers (and subsequently parents) struggle with. Sheri Van Dijk offers tangible tools to deal with emotional upheaval, volatile emotions, and difficult relationships. The exercises that Van Dijk includes in each chapter will assist teens by offering them options for coping with their emotions. Having raised three teenagers, I strongly believe these skills should be taught in schools as part of the curriculum!"

—**Kathy Christie, ADR,** mental health case manager at York Support Services Network in Newmarket, ON, Canada

"Van Dijk has written a workbook that any teen struggling with emotions will find very helpful. Using clear and concise language, this workbook offers awareness-enhancing exercises and practical help for recognizing, sorting out, and changing the way painful emotions can be handled. I found this book useful and easy to read, and I will recommend it to my teenage patients."

—**Mark R. Katz, MD, FRCOP(C),** staff psychiatrist at the Southlake Regional Health Centre. and assistant professor at the University of Toronto

"I highly recommend this well-written, user-friendly workbook written especially for teens. It provides easy-to-use tools for harnessing unruly emotions and calming uncontrolled thinking. By following the suggestions in this workbook, teens will feel more capable of controlling their mood, have more harmonious relationships, gain confidence, and live happier lives."

—**Linda Jeffery, RN,** cognitive behavior therapist in private practice in Newmarket, ON, Canada

"Emotions are generally undervalued in Western society. Many of us receive negative messages about emotions and come to experience them as worthless, problematic, or dangerous. However, emotions are powerful motivators and valid sources of knowledge. Van Dijk addresses these, and other important issues, in this book. She presents information about a range of emotional issues in an accessible manner. She also includes activities that will help deepen the reader's understanding and integration of the material."

—**Karma Guindon, MSW, RSW, RMFT**

"Strongly recommended for teens whose moods interfere with their ability to enjoy life and relationships. Van Dijk has presented Linehan's DBT skills in a manner that is user-friendly and easy to understand. Van Dijk first describes why these skills can be useful, then presents exercises that give the reader an opportunity to practice the skills."

—**Marilyn Becker, MSW, RSW,** clinical supervisor at Addiction Services for York Region

I dedicate this book to my clients: your courage is inspiring and accompanying you on your journey is an honor.

And as always to my family: thank you for your love, support, and encouragement.

Introduction

Something about this book caught your attention—maybe you've been feeling sad a lot lately; maybe you're finding yourself snapping at the people you care about; or perhaps you've noticed that you've recently been feeling more anxious or nervous. Whatever emotional issues you're dealing with, this workbook can help. The main goal of this book is to help you learn to manage your emotions so that they don't get the better of you and make you do things you end up regretting.

So what does it mean to manage your emotions? We all have emotions; they're a necessary part of being human, and we wouldn't want to get rid of them even if we could. Learning to manage your emotions means becoming more aware of your feelings and figuring out what to do with them so that you're not hurting yourself or other people because of how you feel. It means learning to put up with your emotions, even when they're painful, instead of trying to avoid them.

Think about how you deal with your emotions right now. Do you let yourself feel them or do you fight them? Do you avoid them? Do you drink or use drugs to try to escape them? Do you lash out at people you care about because you're in pain and you don't know what else to do to help yourself feel better? Or maybe you use humor to try to hide from your feelings and prevent others from seeing that you're really hurting inside.

Whatever techniques you're using to try to not feel your emotions or to cope with how you're feeling, they're probably not working, or you wouldn't be looking at this workbook. This book will teach you the skills you need to manage your emotions in a healthy way. When you can do that, you'll see that you'll feel better about yourself, and your relationships will go more smoothly. You'll be able to live a healthier, more balanced life where your emotions are no longer in control. In addition to the skills found in this workbook, there are materials available for download at this book's website: http://www.newharbinger.com/47360. (See the very back of this book for more details.)

Dialectical behavior therapy (DBT) is a treatment that was created by Dr. Marsha Linehan (1993), a psychologist in Seattle, Washington. She developed this therapy to help people who had a really hard time regulating their emotions (also known as *emotion dysregulation*). Quite often, people with this type of emotional problem end up hurting themselves physically, or at the very least, they do things that actually cause them more problems—like using drugs or alcohol, shoplifting, gambling, or having unprotected sex and multiple partners. They tend to lead chaotic lives because their emotions are often so out of control, which can lead to problems in their relationships. You might have noticed some of these consequences in your own life and that your inability to manage your emotions sometimes leads to problems at school, at work, and with the law.

This workbook will teach you the DBT skills you need to help you live a healthier, less-confusing life. These skills are separated into four categories. The first, *mindfulness* skills, will help you get to know yourself better and have more choice over how you respond to your emotions and how you act in situations. In the second set of skills, *emotion regulation,* you will learn important information about your emotions that will help you manage them better and increase the pleasurable emotions in your life. *Distress tolerance* skills will help you get through crisis situations without making things worse by falling back on problematic behaviors you may have used in the past, like drinking, avoiding things, or throwing temper tantrums. The final set of skills, *interpersonal effectiveness,* will help you develop healthier relationships with other people.

So before you read further, take a closer look at yourself and decide what you think you need to change. Following is a list of behaviors that are sorted into the four sets of DBT skills. Check off each of the following statements that apply to you. If you notice that you have more checks in certain sections, this will be the set of skills you will want to be especially focused on as you work your way through this book.

Mindfulness

☐ I often say or do things without thinking and later regret my words or actions.

☐ I usually feel like I don't really know who I am, what I like and dislike, and what my values are.

☐ I often go along with the beliefs and values of others so that I won't feel different.

☐ I sometimes feel bad or upset without knowing exactly what I'm feeling or why.

☐ I often judge myself or other people critically.

☐ I frequently try to avoid things that make me uncomfortable.

☐ I often find myself saying things like "This shouldn't have happened," "It's not fair," or "It's not right."

Emotion Regulation

☐ I try to avoid my emotions by sleeping, partying a lot, immersing myself in video games, or doing other things that take me away from my feelings.

☐ Emotions are scary for me. I try to push them away or get rid of them in other ways.

☐ I tend to dwell on the things I don't like about my life.

☐ I am not very active and don't regularly do activities that I enjoy.

☐ I neglect setting short- or long-term goals for myself; for example, I avoid thinking about where I'd like to be in a year, in two years, or in five years.

☐ I often don't have events or situations coming up in my life to look forward to.

Distress Tolerance

☐ I regularly dwell on painful things that have happened to me.

☐ I often find myself having painful emotions because I think about things that have happened in the past or that might happen in the future.

☐ I tend to ignore my own needs; for example, I don't usually take the time to do things that are relaxing, soothing, or enjoyable for me.

☐ When I'm in crisis, I often find myself making the situation worse by doing problematic things like drinking or using drugs, lashing out at others who are trying to help, and so on.

☐ I tend to lose friends or the support of my family because they don't like the things I do to cope with my emotions.

Interpersonal Effectiveness

☐ I feel like I give or take more in my relationships rather than having a balance of give *and* take.

☐ I often feel taken advantage of in relationships.

☐ When relationships aren't going well, I tend to end them without first trying to fix the problems.

☐ I often struggle to keep relationships in my life.

☐ I tend to be more passive in communicating with others; for example, I don't stick up for myself or I go along with the other person all the time.

☐ I tend to be more aggressive in communication with others; for example, I try to force my opinion on the other person.

☐ I tend to get into relationships with others who do unhealthy things, like use drugs or drink a lot, or who get into a lot of trouble with their parents or even with the police, or with people who don't treat me well or who bully me.

Each of the check marks indicates an area you need to work on. You may also have some other ideas about how you would like to change your life. In the following space, write down any ideas you have about what else you would like to do differently in your life:

Now that you have some ideas about the specific things you would like to work on improving in your life, let's start to look at some skills that can help get you there.

CHAPTER ONE

Mindfulness: Learning Self-Awareness

Mindfulness is about living your life in a way that most of us aren't used to. It's about paying close attention to what you're doing in the present moment, noticing when your attention wanders, and bringing it back to what you're doing. It's also about accepting, or not judging, whatever you happen to notice in the present moment, whether it's thoughts you're having, emotions that are coming up, things that are distracting you, or whatever.

Have you ever noticed how hard it can be to concentrate and how frustrated you can get, for example, when you're trying to do your homework but the house is noisy because your little brother is running around wild? Or maybe you're trying to talk on the phone to a friend, and your parents keep interrupting you to ask questions about school or if you got your chores done? Distractions are part of life, but sometimes they make it harder to get things done, and sometimes they can get you feeling so overwhelmed that you just can't manage your emotions.

Mindfulness is a skill that is helpful in many ways. It can help you concentrate better; it can help improve your memory; it can help you get to know yourself better as you become more aware of what you're thinking and feeling. Mindfulness can help you reduce your stress level; it can improve your physical health; and it can help you sleep better. Mindfulness is also really helpful with emotional problems that people sometimes experience, like feeling anxious, angry, or depressed.

In this workbook, we're going to focus on using mindfulness as one skill to help you manage your emotions more effectively. Mindfulness can help you manage yourself and your emotions better so that you will be more able to choose how to act in situations instead of just reacting.

Mindfulness and Your Thoughts

The idea that you are often not aware of what you're thinking might seem rather strange, but consider it for a minute: Have you ever had someone ask what you were thinking about and realized that you weren't actually sure? Do you ever suddenly notice when you're reading a book or watching television that your attention has drifted and you have no idea what's going on in the book or the TV program? The fact is, we're often not paying attention to what we're thinking about—usually, we let our minds wander wherever they want to go without paying much attention to them and without trying to control them. This can cause problems.

Imagine you're sitting in class. Your teacher is talking, and you find it really hard to concentrate on what she's saying. So instead of trying to focus, you just let your thoughts drift off and you start to think about whom you're going to sit with at lunch, about the fight you had yesterday with your best friend, or about what you're going to do this weekend. Your mind jumps from one thing to another. Maybe you get caught up in a daydream for a while about what it will be like after you graduate and you don't have to sit through these boring classes anymore but can go out and get a job and live on your own. While all these thoughts are going on, while your mind is wandering from place to place, taking you along for the ride, for the most part, you probably aren't very aware of what you're thinking about—not to mention the fact that you've just missed your teacher's instructions for the next test.

The Consequences of Being Unmindful

This is how most of us live much of our lives—with our minds taking us wherever they want to go. Our minds tend to control us, instead of the other way around. They flit from the past to the future; then they might come back to the present for a while before launching back into thoughts about things other than what we're doing right now.

Think for a moment about how this affects you. If you're doing one thing but thinking about something else, what happens? You might be able to come up with a few possible outcomes: your memory isn't as good when you're not fully focusing on what you're doing; or you might make more mistakes when you're not thinking about the task at hand. But the most important consequences, for the purpose of this workbook, are the emotional ones. If you're not thinking about the present, you must be thinking about the past or the future. And when you're thinking about the past or the future, you're likely not thinking about happy things—instead, the tendency is to think about things that trigger painful emotions. Thinking about the past, you may notice that you start to feel sad, angry, ashamed, and so on, about things that have happened, things you've done, or things that others have done to you. Likewise, thinking about the future tends to trigger anxiety. *Anxiety* is that sense of fear, or intense worry or nervousness, that often goes along with uncomfortable physical sensations. For example, you may notice that you get the jitters or butterflies in your stomach, or that your heart starts to race or flutter, while you're worrying that things might go wrong.

Living in the past or the future is the opposite of mindfulness. Mindfulness is about living in the present moment, with awareness and with acceptance—realizing that things are okay just as they are, right now in this moment. In other words, it's about focusing on what you're doing in the here and now, not judging whatever is happening, and bringing your attention back when your thoughts wander from what you're doing in the present. This probably sounds pretty complicated, and it's definitely not how most of us are used to living our lives, so let's look at an example to help make sense of this idea.

Jacob's Story

Jacob had been invited to a party at a friend's house. At first he was happy he had been invited and was looking forward to the party, but as the party got closer, Jacob began to think about what it might be like. He thought about the last time he had gone to a party; some people there had made fun of him, embarrassing him in front of his friends. Thinking about those past events made Jacob angry and brought back the embarrassment and shame all over again. It also made him start to worry that the upcoming party would be like the last one, and he got anxious about going.

Jacob went to the party, but the entire time he was worrying that something was going to happen like the last time and that he would

> end up looking foolish again. He missed out on a lot of the fun, because he was so caught up thinking about the past and worrying about the future that he was too distracted to enjoy a lot of what was happening in the present moment.

The present might not be wonderful and full of happy emotions, but think of it this way: if you're living in the present moment, you have to deal only with what's actually going on in that moment. If you're not living in the present, you still have to deal with whatever's happening in the present moment, and you also have to deal with the emotions being brought up by the thoughts you're having about the past or the future. It's like bouncing between three realities at once, which can be exhausting.

Mindfulness has you noticing how you're feeling, acknowledging it, and then focusing on what's going on for you in the moment. If Jacob had been practicing mindfulness about the party, it might have looked something like this:

> Jacob had been invited to a party at a friend's house. At first he was happy he had been invited and was looking forward to it, but as the party got closer, Jacob noticed that he had started to worry about what the party might be like. He noticed that his thoughts kept turning to the last time he had gone to

a party, when some people there had made fun of him, embarrassing him in front of his friends. Jacob also noticed that whenever he started to think about those past events, he began to get angry, embarrassed, and ashamed all over again. It also made him start to worry that the upcoming party would be like the last one, and he got anxious about going.

Being aware of these things, Jacob went to the party and focused on being mindful while he was there: being in the moment, with awareness and with acceptance. Sometimes he would start to worry that something was going to happen like the last time and that he would end up looking foolish again, but as soon as he noticed the worry and the thoughts that were triggering it, he would bring himself back to the present moment and would really focus on what was happening then and there. He would say to himself, *I notice I'm feeling anxious. My palms are sweaty and my heart is racing.* He'd then take a deep breath and bring his attention back to whatever was happening in the present: *There's nothing bad happening to me right now. I'm here with my friends.*

Jacob found he really had to work at it at first, but as the night went on, he was able to relax more, spending less time having to focus on his straying thoughts and more time enjoying himself.

Mindfulness can be really helpful in many different ways, but it's also pretty hard to practice, especially when you first start. You might have noticed in Jacob's story that he was working on being aware of his thoughts and his present experience. Most of us aren't used to being this aware, and it can take a lot of work. To help you with this, you'll be practicing different mindfulness exercises throughout this book. The following exercise will help you start thinking about how mindfulness can be helpful in your life.

1 How Aware Are You of Your Thoughts?

It's important for you to think about your current patterns or habits, so you can then think about what you need to change. Over the next few days, do your best to notice where your thoughts tend to wander to: Do you think about the past a lot? Do you often find yourself living in the future? Are there certain themes your mind keeps returning to? Write about whatever you notice here:

_____
_____
_____

Have you noticed that your thoughts tend to wander more in certain situations or when you're doing certain things? If so, in which situations or activities does your mind tend to wander?

_____

When your thoughts have wandered from the present moment, what emotions tend to come up for you? Write anything you've noticed here:

_____

_____

2 How Unmindful Thoughts Can Trigger Painful Emotions

Read the following stories. Keeping in mind that living in the past or the future is likely to trigger more painful emotions, see if you can identify the person in each story as being mindful (that is, focused on the present moment with acceptance) or unmindful (not focused on the present; possibly judging the situation). Circle whichever word seems to be most accurate; you'll find a list of answers at the end of the book.

1. Stacey was talking to her friend about a problem she was having with her parents. When she had finished telling the story,

which she was quite angry over, her friend said she thought Stacey was being silly and should just get over it, that lots of other people had bigger problems than Stacey did. Stacey was stunned, and she thought, *I can't believe she just said that. I'm feeling really hurt and angry right now. I'm having an urge to say something really hurtful back to her.*

Mindful   Unmindful

2. Kevin was sitting in his room, feeling really angry and sad. He was thinking about what had happened earlier that day—he had overheard his friend Toby talking, and he was pretty sure that Toby was talking about him. Kevin thought, *I can't believe that Toby said those mean things about me. This always ends up happening to me; people who used to be my friends turn on me. I'll never have friends I can trust.*

Mindful   Unmindful

3. Jessica was discussing curfew with her parents and was getting really upset because they wouldn't budge on her regular ten o'clock time, even though she was going to a school dance that would be chaperoned. She tuned out her parents and thought,

Blah blah blah ... They never trust me. They always insist on treating me like a child.

Mindful   Unmindful

4. Mark was sitting in class and was getting quite frustrated because two girls behind him kept whispering. He thought, *I'm having a really hard time focusing right now because people are talking, and I'm starting to feel frustrated.*

Mindful   Unmindful

5. Sarah was at a party with a bunch of friends from school. All her friends were talking to each other and having a good time, but Sarah found herself alone in the living room, watching television. She thought, *I always feel so anxious when I'm at parties, but everyone else looks comfortable. What's wrong with me? I'll never fit in.*

Mindful   Unmindful

6. Tyler had been working on the same skateboard trick for quite a while and still hadn't gotten it down. He was getting closer but had just fallen off his board for what seemed like the millionth time. He thought, *I've been working on this trick for*

quite a while. Sometimes it gets frustrating, but I'm going to keep at it.

Mindful   Unmindful

3 Mindfulness Breathing

Now that you have more of an understanding of what it means to be mindful, it's time to actually practice a mindfulness exercise. For the next few moments, just focus on your breath. Don't change the way you're breathing; just notice how it feels to breathe. Notice the feel of the air as it enters your nostrils; notice your belly expanding as the air inflates your lungs. Simply pay attention to whatever you notice about how it feels to breathe. At some point, you'll likely become aware that your attention has wandered: maybe you'll start thinking that this seems weird and wondering what the point is; maybe you'll get distracted by sounds; perhaps your thoughts will wander to lunchtime, wondering what you're going to eat. Whatever comes to your attention, just notice it; then, without judging yourself for wandering, and without judging whatever you're experiencing, bring your attention back to your breath. Do this for about a minute or so, and then answer the following questions about your experience.

What did you notice while you were focusing on your breath?

_____
_____
_____
_____
_____

Were you paying attention to your breath the whole time or did your attention wander? If it wandered, where did your thoughts go?

_____
_____

Did you accept whatever came to your awareness? For example, if you noticed yourself being distracted by a barking dog, did you just accept it *(I hear a dog barking)* or did you find yourself judging it in some way *(That barking dog is really annoying)*? Or perhaps you noticed your attention wandered a lot; did you accept this *(I'm really having a hard time staying focused right now)* or did you judge yourself for this *(I can't even do this right!)*? Write about anything you noticed here:

_____
_____
_____
_____

It's normal for your attention to wander, so as best you can, don't judge yourself when this happens—accept it, and bring your attention back to your breath. We'll be looking more at judgments and acceptance in chapter 4, so if it doesn't quite make sense yet, don't worry—it will!

For now, this might help: Think of your mind as a puppy being trained to sit and stay. When you first start to teach that puppy, it's not going to listen to you. Then it will start to catch on and will stay for a few seconds before straying again; as time goes on, it will get better and better at staying when you tell it to. Your mind will behave in the same way—it's never been trained to stay before! So you might need to bring your attention back again, and again in just one minute, and that's okay. You wouldn't get impatient and angry at the puppy when it doesn't stay, because you know it's just learning, so be patient with yourself as well. Remember to accept whatever you happen to notice and bring your attention back to the present moment, without judgment.

Since mindfulness is about returning to the present moment when your attention wanders and accepting whatever you become aware of, you can do absolutely anything mindfully. So if you're listening to music mindfully, you are just listening to the music, not judging it, and bringing your attention back whenever it wanders from the song you're listening to. If you're cleaning your bedroom mindfully, you are focused on just doing that one thing; when you notice your attention wanders, don't judge yourself for wandering, but just bring your attention back. When you notice that you're judging your mom for making you clean your room, notice that, and bring your attention back.

Here are some other activities you can do mindfully. Add your own ideas on the blank lines.
Reading a book
Talking to a friend
Watching TV or a movie
Skateboarding
Paying attention in class
Scrolling through your Instagram feed
Rollerblading
Dancing
Playing with a pet
Doing your chores
Doing your homework
Taking a walk

If you had a hard time thinking of activities you can do mindfully, think about things you really enjoy doing. Starting to practice mindfulness will be a bit easier if you begin with activities that you're able to throw yourself into. The eventual goal is to live your life more mindfully, so from here you'll move on to doing other things mindfully as well.

Mindfulness and Your Emotions

You might be wondering what listening to music or cleaning your room has to do with your emotions. Remember that when you're not in the present moment (in the here and now), you're often triggering painful emotions for yourself. So when you're listening to music, for example, you might find that the music reminds you of something (like a past relationship or someone you like who's dating someone else) and get caught up in those thoughts and memories. When you're living outside the immediate present in this way, you actually experience the emotions as if you were going through that event again—maybe not to the same degree, but you still have those same emotions.

You probably have enough going on in the present that brings up painful emotions for you, without bringing up stuff from the past. Listening to music, cleaning your room, or doing anything else mindfully means that you are bringing your attention back to the present moment instead of letting your mind take you wherever it wants to go. This helps you manage your emotions more effectively in two ways. First, by being mindful, you're preventing painful emotions from being triggered by thoughts of the past or worries about the future. In this way, mindfulness reduces the number and intensity of emotions you experience regularly. Second, when you're not judging, you'll also have less emotional pain coming up, and when you have fewer emotions on an ongoing basis, they're going to be more manageable.

In your mind, picture a bucket full of water. It's full right up to the brim so that adding even one more drop of water is going to make it overflow. Now imagine that the bucket represents your emotions.

When you're walking around full of emotions to begin with, because you're angry, sad, ashamed, or anxious about the past or the future, adding just one more painful emotion, even a small one, can make you overflow emotionally. This overflowing can mean different things for different people or even for the same person at different times. For example, you might explode at your mom for asking you to clean up your room; you might have the urge to hurt yourself because your best friend had to cancel your plans to go to a party; or you might get to a point where you feel so depressed that you stop getting out of bed to go to school. The point is, mindfulness helps you reduce the number and intensity of emotions in your bucket, so you'll be more able to manage the emotions that are there.

4 Your Bucket of Emotions

Draw a water line across the bucket where you think your emotional level is right now; for example, if your emotional level is quite low right now, you might draw the line below the halfway point; if it's high, you might put it at the top of the bucket. After you've drawn your line, think about what emotions are present for you right now and write their names in the blanks provided. If you're not sure what emotions you're feeling, you may need to come back to this exercise after completing chapter 2. If you're able to fill in the blanks now, do so, and then answer the questions that follow.

How did it feel to name your emotions during this exercise?

Did you notice anything about your emotions as you were naming them? For example, did you begin to experience more emotions or fewer?

Now write some notes about your emotions, in general. For example, do you think your bucket tends to overflow or do you think it's usually at a manageable level? Are you often aware of your emotions or do you tend to ignore them?

Mindfulness and Your Physical Sensations

Have you ever noticed that emotions usually come with physical sensations? For example, when you're feeling sad, you might notice that your throat gets tight, your eyes get watery, and you have the urge to cry. Or when you're angry, you might notice that you become flushed, your heart starts to beat faster, and your muscles tighten up.

Our physical sensations can often be a really good indicator of how we feel emotionally. Being mindful of our physical sensations, therefore, can help us be more aware of our emotions, which increases our ability to manage them. The first step is to become familiar with how your emotions feel in your body.

5 How Do Your Emotions Feel?

Write about how each of these emotions feels for you physically. For example, does your heart speed up, do you feel tightness in certain areas of your body, or do you tend to clench certain body parts? You might need to experience each of these emotions again before you can accurately describe what happens, so do what you can now and come back to this exercise later if necessary.

Anger
_____
_____
_____

Happiness
_____

Fear/Anxiety
_____

Sadness

_____
_____

Guilt/Shame
_____
_____
_____

6 Mindfulness to Physical Sensations

The following mindfulness practice is called a *body scan*, because it has you slowly scan your body by muscle groups to see where you feel relaxed, have tension or pain, or experience other sensations. By being more in tune with how your body feels, you can often increase your awareness of your emotions, which in turn increases your ability to manage them. You might want to try having someone read the following instructions out loud to you until you get used to doing this on your own.

Begin by getting yourself into a comfortable seated position and tuning into your breath. Don't try to change your breath, but just notice it; feel your body as you inhale and exhale. When you're ready, turn your attention to your feet, allowing yourself to notice your toes, the balls of your feet, and your heels. Observe how your feet feel surrounded by the shoes or socks you're wearing; or if you're barefoot, you might notice the feel of the floor and the difference in temperature on the bottom of your feet compared to the top. Just let yourself become aware of any sensations that are there in this moment; and if you notice nothing at all, that's okay—just notice that.

From here, slowly start to move your attention upward, into your lower legs, your calves and shins; continue to allow yourself to observe, without judging as best as you can, even if what you notice isn't what you would like it to be. Continue to scan your body, one muscle group at a time, as you work your way upward from your feet to your head, noticing any sensations of pain, comfort, discomfort, tension, or relaxation, or anything else that comes to your awareness. Notice that there are no judgments happening here. You're just describing factually whatever you notice in each body part. As you do this, you'll likely notice that your thoughts wander to something else. Remember that this is natural, and just bring your attention back to the muscles you're focusing on.

As you focus on each muscle group, just name the body part to yourself and notice any sensations; for example, *I notice my toes ... have no sensations. I notice my feet ... are a little sore. I notice my calves ... just feel relaxed. I notice my shins ... have no sensations. I notice my quadriceps*

... are feeling tense. Continue to work your way up your body.

Moving upward from your lower legs, focus on your hamstrings, quadriceps, and your buttocks. Slowly continuing upward, bring your attention to your lower, middle, and upper back, pausing at each of these groups of muscles to give yourself time to observe any sensations. From here, notice your shoulders, then slowly work your way down your arms, simply allowing your awareness to come to any sensations that are in your body in this moment. Observe your biceps, elbows, and forearms, and slowly work your way into your wrists, your hands, and down to the ends of each fingertip.

Continue to just sense whatever is happening in your body, without judgment, even if it's not what you would like it to be. Now become aware of your stomach; this is a place people often hold tension, so notice if your abdominal muscles are tight or if they feel relaxed. You can also take a moment to pay attention to your breathing here, noticing if it's deep and regular, shallow, or erratic. Now move your attention upward into your chest, again noticing any tightness or other sensations. Whenever you notice that your attention has wandered, just observe this, accept it (don't judge yourself for it), and bring your attention back to the area you're observing.

Moving your awareness now into your neck, notice any tension, pain, discomfort, or other sensations—just become aware of them. Then move on to your jaw, another place people often hold tension—are you clenching your jaw, or is it loose and relaxed? Just observe whatever is happening in your jaw at this moment. Now draw your awareness to the rest of your face and observe what's happening there. Is your brow furrowed? Are your eyes open or closed, squinting or relaxed? Are the corners of your mouth slightly upturned or downturned? Is there tension in any of these muscles? Finally, bring your attention to your head. You might feel a tingling sensation as the energy flows through your body; or maybe there are no sensations there for you to sense right now, and that's fine too—just observe anything that is there in this moment.

Did you notice anything that you weren't aware of in your body? Were you able to identify any emotions? Practicing this body scan regularly will help you become more in tune with yourself, and with how you feel physically, which can give you clues as to how you feel emotionally.

Mindfulness and Your Values

Most people are able to get to know themselves better as they get older—what they like and dislike, what their beliefs and values are, what's important to them, and so on. This takes some time to sort out even under the best of circumstances, where there are others to talk to and give support when things are difficult. But some people grow up in circumstances that make this process even more challenging—for example, developing a mental health problem or dealing with other adverse experiences like physical, emotional, verbal, or sexual abuse; a family member having a physical or mental health condition or addiction; growing up in a family where financial resources are scarce; or growing up as a minority and facing discrimination on a regular basis.

If you grew up in a difficult situation like this, you may not have had the opportunity to figure out who you are. And when you don't have a good sense of your own identity, this can contribute to problems for you in the long term: you may experience a sense of emptiness; or you may feel as though you don't belong and find yourself doing whatever you can to try to "fit in" with others. This can lead to further problems as you often set aside your own needs to have that experience of belonging. When people don't have a good sense of their own identity, they often become more passive; and this can also result in difficulties in relationships, as resentment builds since they're often not getting their needs met.

The more you practice mindfulness, the more you'll be in tune with your thoughts, physical sensations, and emotions. You'll become more aware of when you're acting in ways that conflict with your values (this can generate a lot of emotional pain, which you'll learn more about when we delve further into emotions in the next chapter).

Let's take some time now to help you consider some of your own values. This next activity is adapted from *The DBT Skills Workbook for Teen Self-Harm* (Van Dijk 2021).

7 What Are Your Values?

Consider your beliefs, or what matters most to you. Is it being successful? Loyal, honest, trustworthy? Physically and emotionally healthy? Being kind to others? You might already have a sense of what some of your values are. If so, list them here:

_____

_____

_____

If you're thinking *I have no idea!* don't worry; try this: bring to mind someone you look up to. It could be a family member or friend; a teacher, coach, guidance counselor, a neighbor or pastor; or it could be someone you've never met, like a political or public figure or a famous person. Now ask yourself, what is it about this person that you admire? What do you see in this person that you would like to be? Write down any words that come to mind here:

_____ _____
_____ _____
_____ _____
_____ _____
_____ _____

If you're still coming up blank, here's a list of things that people often identify as values for them. Check off those that you would say are important to you:
- [ ] Having healthy relationships
- [ ] Being responsible
- [ ] Being healthy
- [ ] Learning
- [ ] Focusing on family
- [ ] Achieving things in life (working hard, getting good grades, being financially secure)
- [ ] Having good character (integrity, honesty, standing up for your beliefs, being respectful)
- [ ] Contributing (volunteering your time, giving back to your community, being generous)
- [ ] Enjoying life
- [ ] Stewardship (such as taking care of the environment)
- [ ] Being part of a group or community
- [ ] Advocating for equality

Now that you've hopefully got some more ideas about what values you might hold, feel free to do some more brainstorming in the following space.

_____
_____
_____
_____

Consider finding a list of values online if you need more ideas.

Now think about the values you've identified, and think about the person you would like to be. Envision yourself living a life worth living (Linehan 1993), where perhaps you have a career or a family, or you're surrounding yourself with people you care about, or you're doing other things that are meaningful to you in some way. Now think about how you tend to act when your emotions are getting the better of you: is this consistent with the values you've listed here? Or does acting from your emotional self often conflict with your values?

Keeping these values in mind as something you're working toward in the long term can help you feel more motivated to put in the work and effort required to build this life for yourself, which means making healthier choices at times (and hopefully more and more as you put the skills you're learning into practice). To help you keep them in mind, you might want to make a photocopy of your list of values and put it somewhere you'll see it as a reminder of these things that are important to you, or draw a picture or make a collage that represents this life you'd like for yourself and hang it on your wall.

Wrapping Up

In this chapter you've learned about a skill called mindfulness and how this skill can help you manage your emotions more effectively. You've also learned that emotions consist of more than just how you feel—they also include thoughts and physical sensations. Before you read any further in this workbook, take some time to practice mindfulness. Use the exercises in this chapter, and as best you can, bring mindfulness to some of the activities you regularly do in your day-to-day life. The more you practice being in the moment, with awareness and acceptance, the more benefit you'll see and the more effectively you'll be able to manage your emotions. If you're interested in learning more about mindfulness, there are numerous resources available (see additional reading suggestions at the end of this workbook).

CHAPTER TWO

What You Need to Know About Emotions

In this chapter, you'll learn information that will continue to increase your ability to manage emotions so that even the intense emotions you experience will have less control over you.

Naming Emotions Can Help You Manage Them

Have you ever noticed that you often don't know what you feel? Do you sometimes feel like you're walking around in an emotional fog, knowing that you feel bad or upset, but not being able to really name the emotion you're feeling? If you don't know what you're feeling, it's really hard to do anything about that emotion or to help yourself tolerate it. Once you can put a name on an emotion, you can often figure out what to do about it. The information in this chapter about emotions comes from Linehan (2014). This next activity is adapted from Van Dijk (2021).

8 Put a Name on It

Probably one reason we get confused about what we're feeling is that we have so many different emotions. This activity will help you look at a few of the more painful emotions that many people struggle with—anger, fear (often experienced as anxiety), sadness, guilt, and shame—but think of this as just a starting point. If you have questions about other emotions that cause problems for you (for some people happiness, joy, love, and other pleasurable emotions can actually be problematic, for example), you'll need to do some more work in this area.

All emotions serve a purpose or can be *justified* at times, which means that they make sense given the situation. We can also feel emotions when they're *not* justified, and this can cause a lot of problems.

Anger

Anger's purpose. Anger is the emotion that usually comes up when there are obstacles in your path or when you or someone you care about is being attacked, threatened, insulted, or hurt by others. When a situation fits into one of these categories, you can say that anger is justified; it makes sense given the situation.

What it does. Anger typically causes people to become aggressive; it might lead you to attack what you see as dangerous to make the threat go away. When the human race was evolving, and there were constant threats in the environment, anger helped us survive.

Example of when anger is justified. Your parents ground you for breaking curfew; they are creating an obstacle that's getting in your way (you can't go to that party you were planning on). Therefore, it makes sense that you would feel angry in this situation; anger is justified.

Anger thoughts. *This isn't fair. They shouldn't be treating me this way. They're being mean. This is stupid.* Usually anger thoughts involve judgments, thinking what's happening shouldn't be happening or people shouldn't be the way they are.

Describe Your Anger

Think of a recent time when you felt angry, and describe the situation:

_____
_____

Body sensations. Take a look at these physical sensations connected to anger, and check off any that you experienced in this situation. Add any other sensations that you can recall:

☐ Tense or tight muscles, such as clenching fists or jaw

☐ Trembling or shaking
☐ Racing heart
☐ Increased breathing rate
☐ Change in body temperature, which might lead to feeling hot or cold
☐ Other: _____

Urges and behavior. Anger usually involves aggression, so you might yell, scream, swear, or say hurtful things to someone, or you might even physically lash out, throw things, or hit or punch things or people (including yourself).

What urges did you notice when you were in the situation you described?

_____
_____

What did you actually do?

_____
_____

Other words for anger. Circle any of these words that describe how you felt in this situation:

Annoyed
Frustrated
Irritated
Exasperated
Resentful
Bitter
Mad

Irate
Furious
Aggravated
Bothered
Enraged
Outraged
Indignant
Impatient

If you can think of another word or words that fit better, add them here.

_____

_____

It's important to note that just because a feeling is justified doesn't mean you have to act on the urges associated with it. For example, you can feel anger at your parents for setting a curfew and choose not to respond to your urge to shout at them.

Fear and Anxiety

Fear is different from but very related to anxiety. Fear motivates you to act when there's a threat; it triggers the fight-or-flight response in your body, which helps you survive in a dangerous situation. Fear and anxiety essentially feel the same physically. The main difference between these two emotions is that fear is present focused and related to a specific threat, while anxiety comes up when there's a more general threat that you are worrying about, something that hasn't happened yet and may never happen. Anxiety will also come up when there's something you might reasonably expect to happen and you expect the results to be catastrophic, out of proportion with reality. So, if you're riding your bike or walking down the road and you're thinking the thought *What if I get hit by a car?* you're likely going to feel anxious. If you're doing a presentation at school and you're thinking *I'm going to make a fool out of myself and fail the whole thing*, you're going to feel anxious. While there are definitely times when fear is justified, there isn't really a time when you *should* feel anxious, or when your anxiety would be justified, because it involves a fear of something that isn't a real threat—even if it feels like it is!

Some anxiety can be helpful, however. Without it, you wouldn't be cautious while crossing the road, so you wouldn't see the car as it comes barreling toward you. Without some anxiety, you might do other things that put you more at risk, like walking alone in an unsafe part of town at night. So we're not trying to get rid of anxiety (or of any emotion, for that matter, since all emotions serve a purpose), but if you have anxiety regularly—or to the extreme, such as having panic attacks—we want you to be able to manage it better, instead of letting it control you.

Fear's purpose. Fear comes up when there is a danger to your safety or your well-being or to that of someone you care about.

What fear does. Fear is the emotion that causes you to act to protect yourself or others.

Example of when fear is justified. You're riding your bike or walking across the road and a car is speeding right toward you. Fear is justified because your safety is threatened.

Describe Your Fear or Anxiety

Think of a recent time when you felt fearful or anxious, and describe the situation:

_____
_____

Body sensations. Take a look at these physical sensations that can be connected to fear and anxiety, and check off those that you experienced in this situation. Then add any other sensations that you experienced:

☐ Tense or tight muscles (your body preparing you to flee a dangerous situation)
☐ Trembling or shaking muscles
☐ Racing heart
☐ Increased breathing rate
☐ Change in body temperature, which might lead to feeling hot or cold
☐ Other: _____

Urges and behaviors. With fear, urges and behaviors usually involve running away from the threat to protect yourself or the people you care about. With anxiety, this usually means avoiding a situation (like when you decide not to go to class, because you're worried that you'll have a panic attack and make a fool of yourself) or escaping the situation if you're already in it (like leaving class early because you're feeling anxious).

What urges did you notice when you were in the situation you described?

_____

_____

What did you actually do?

_____

_____

Other words for fear. Circle any of these words that describe how you felt in this situation:

Anxious
Panicky
Terrified
Scared
Afraid
Apprehensive
Nervous
Worried
Dread

Disturbed
Stressed
Tense
Frantic
Overwhelmed
Alarmed
Disconcerted

If you can think of another word or words that fit better, add them here.

_____

_____

As you recalled your experience of fear or anxiety, did you notice any similarity to what you experienced when feeling angry? The body sensations can be similar. This is why it can be easy to mix up feelings of anxiety and anger!

Sadness

Purpose of Sadness. Sadness is the emotion felt when things aren't the way you expected them to be or when you've experienced a loss of some sort.

What it does. This is the emotion that encourages people around you to try to be of help or offer support; it might also motivate you to try to regain what you've lost.

Example of when sadness is justified. Your best friend is in Europe for six months on a soccer scholarship, or you don't get into your first choice of colleges, or your significant other breaks up with you. Sadness is justified because you've experienced loss, even if only temporary, and because things aren't as you had expected them to be.

Describe Your Sadness

Think of a recent time when you felt sad, and describe the situation:

_____
_____
_____

Body sensations. Take a look at these physical sensations connected to sadness, and check off the ones you experienced in this situation. Then add any other sensations that you experienced:

☐ Tightness in chest or throat
☐ Heaviness in chest or heart
☐ Tears in eyes
☐ Tired or heavy body
☐ Other: _____

Urges and behaviors. Feeling sad usually involves withdrawing from others and isolating.

What urges did you notice when you were in the situation you described?

_____
_____

What did you actually do?

_____
_____

Other words for sadness. Circle any of these words that describe how you felt in this situation:

    Disappointed
    Discouraged
    Distraught
    Resigned
    Hopeless
    Miserable
    Despair
    Grief
    Sorrow
    Anguish
    Down
    Distressed
    Heartbroken
    Glum
    Depressed

If you can think of another word or words that fit your feelings better, add them here.

_____
_____

Guilt

We often feel guilt and shame in the same situations, and many aspects of these emotions are similar. They're easy to confuse but are quite different; and it's important to know that we often experience these emotions when they're not actually justified, so they can cause us a lot of unnecessary suffering.

Guilt's purpose. Guilt is the feeling that comes up when you've done something that goes against your values and you judge your behavior.

What it does. Guilt comes up to help you make amends and to prevent you from acting like this in the future.

Examples of when guilt is justified. You say something to hurt your sister during an argument, and later you think, *That was a low blow. I shouldn't have said that.* You lie to your parents or cheat on a test, and there's part of you that knows the behavior doesn't match with your values, so you feel guilty about it.

Describe Your Guilt

Think of a recent time when you felt guilt and describe the situation here:

_____
_____

Body sensations. Take a look at these body sensations connected to guilt, and check off the ones that you experienced in this situation. Then add any other sensations that you experienced:

- ☐ Feeling and acting jittery, nervous
- ☐ Hot, flushed face
- ☐ Other: _____

Urges and behaviors. When feeling guilty, you often want to make amends (apologizing to your sister, for example) to try to make up for what you did. There's usually also an urge to bow your head and avoid eye contact.

What urges did you notice when you were in the situation you described?
_____
_____

What did you actually do?
_____
_____

Other words for guilt. Circle any of these words that describe how you felt in this situation:

Remorseful

Apologetic

Regretful

Sorry

If you can think of another word or words that fit your feelings better, add them here.

_____

Shame

Shame's purpose. Shame protects you by keeping you connected to others. Shame comes up when you've done something or when there is something about you as a person that could cause a person (or group of people) to reject you if they knew about it.

What it does. Shame causes you to hide—either yourself or your behavior—so that you can remain connected to people who are important to you. Shame is also the emotion that comes up to try to stop you from doing the same behavior again. If people know about your behavior, shame causes you to try to make amends in those relationships.

Examples of when shame is justified. You cut yourself, and you hide the cuts so that others won't reject you for this behavior. Whether or not shame is justified in this example actually depends on who you're hiding from: if you're hiding your behavior from people who might reject you for cutting, then it's justified, because hiding the behavior keeps you connected to others. But shame is not justified if you're feeling this way around people who will probably not reject you—people like your parents, your best friend, or your therapist.

You may also experience this emotion if there's something about you that makes you different from others, or at least you believe it makes you different. This could be your sexuality or gender identity, a mental health or addiction problem, your religion, or a particular belief or opinion you hold. Hiding that part of yourself protects you from being rejected by others. It's sometimes difficult to tell if shame is justified or not, because it involves an evaluation of others and what they might think if they knew about this thing.

More often than not, shame isn't justified. It often comes up, though, because shame is the awful, soul-sucking feeling that we feel when we judge ourselves. So instead of thinking *I shouldn't have said that to my sister*, you're now thinking *What kind of person am I that I would say that to my sister?* or *I'm awful*. Judging yourself for something you've done or for something you feel is defective or wrong about you will cause you to feel shame.

One reason you may tend to confuse guilt and shame is that you can feel both at the same time, when you judge your behavior (guilt) and then you judge yourself for having done that behavior (shame).

Describe Your Shame

Think of a recent time when you felt shame, and describe the situation here:

_____
_____
_____

Body sensations. Take a look at these physical sensations connected to shame, and check off the ones you experienced in this situation. Then add any other sensations that you experienced:

- ☐ Pain in the pit of the stomach
- ☐ Hot, flushed face
- ☐ Difficulty making eye contact
- ☐ Other: _____

Urges and behaviors. Shame can make you want to crawl under the nearest rock; it can be difficult to make eye contact. It can create an urge to isolate yourself and hide from others, leading to slumped posture and bowed head.

What urges did you notice when you were in the situation you described?

_____
_____

What did you actually do?

_____
_____

Other words for shame. Circle any of these words that describe how you felt in this situation:

Mortified

Self-loathing

Self-disgust

If you can think of another word or words that fit your feelings better, add them here.

_____

_____

There aren't really many other words for shame, although sometimes we use the words "embarrassed" or "humiliated," which are both different from shame. You can think of *embarrassed* as the feeling you have when you walk out of the bathroom with TP stuck to your foot—embarrassing situations we can usually laugh at later. *Humiliation* is a little closer to shame, but it also involves anger—the sense of someone having caused you to feel shame when you didn't deserve it.

The Job of Emotions

As you saw from the previous activity, emotions come up for a reason—they all have jobs. Whenever you experience an emotion, it's there to tell you something. For example, anger often comes up to motivate us to work toward change when there's something we don't like about a situation; fear and anxiety come up when there's something that could be dangerous to us, motivating us to leave the situation or protect ourselves; and so on. But sometimes people become more emotionally sensitive, which means that their emotions get triggered more often than they need to. You might find you get angry over something that seems small and wouldn't normally bother you, or maybe you feel anxious in a situation where there really isn't anything that's threatening to you. Still, you can usually see why the emotion has come up in you, even if you think it's an overreaction. So the point is not to try to get rid of your emotions—you need them; instead, you want to be able to manage them more effectively and not let them control you.

9 What's This Emotion Telling You?

These short stories demonstrate how our emotions all have jobs. Read each story and answer the questions that follow. You'll find a list of possible answers at the end of the book.

Kayla's parents had split up when she was twelve, and her father had recently remarried. Kayla didn't like the way Mary, his new wife, treated her—she was often critical of Kayla, and it seemed like she was trying to be Kayla's mother. One day after school, Kayla left her report card on the kitchen table for her father to see. She was proud of herself for having gotten a B in math, a class she had always struggled with. Mary looked at Kayla's report card before her father could see it and told Kayla she was going to have to work a lot harder, because Bs were not acceptable.

Circle the emotion that best describes what Kayla might feel:

Anger   Anxiety   Sadness   Guilt   Shame

What might the job of this emotion be? What's it telling Kayla?

_____
_____

What helpful action might Kayla take because of this emotion?

_____
_____

Joshua and his girlfriend Emily had been dating for a few months. Things had been going well until the last week or so, when Joshua started to notice that Emily wasn't calling or texting him as often. They didn't get to see each other much during the week because Joshua had a part-time job after school and Emily often had volleyball practice. Joshua had been looking forward to spending time with Emily this weekend, but Emily hadn't responded to his text, and he was starting to wonder if she was going to break up with him.

Circle the emotion that best describes what Joshua might feel:

Anger   Anxiety   Sadness   Guilt   Shame

What might the job of this emotion be? What's it telling Joshua?

_____
_____

What helpful action might Joshua take because of this emotion?

_____
_____

Nicole had an argument with her best friend, Samantha, and they stopped talking to each other. A week went by, and Samantha still hadn't called, but Nicole didn't want to be the one to give in. Instead of going to the party they had planned to go to on the weekend, Nicole stayed home and watched movies by herself. She just didn't feel like doing anything with anyone else right now.

Circle the emotion that best describes what Nicole might feel:

Anger   Anxiety   Sadness   Guilt   Shame

What might the job of this emotion be? What's it telling Nicole?

_____

_____

What helpful action might Nicole take because of this emotion?

_____

_____

Matt had broken curfew twice last week, and now he was grounded. As part of his punishment, his cell phone had been taken away. It was Saturday night and he was bored; his parents had gone to visit friends, so he went into their room and took his mom's cell phone so he could text some friends. He fell asleep without returning the phone, and the next morning his mom asked if he had seen it. Matt said he hadn't because he didn't want to get into more trouble and be grounded for even longer.

Circle the emotion that best describes what Matt might feel:

Anger   Anxiety   Sadness   Guilt   Shame

What might the job of this emotion be? What's it telling Matt?

_____
_____

What helpful action might Matt take because of this emotion?

_____
_____

Can you recall a time you've experienced each of the following emotions? Take some time to reflect on the job it served and what you did because of it, and write about your experiences in the space provided:

A time I felt angry: _____
_____

The job of this emotion: _____
_____

What helpful action I took: _____
_____

A time I felt anxious: _____
The job of this emotion: _____
_____

What helpful action I took: _____

A time I felt sad: _____

The job of this emotion: _____

What helpful action I took: _____

A time I felt guilty: _____

The job of this emotion: _____

What helpful action I took: _____

A time I felt shame: _____

The job of this emotion: _____

What helpful action I took: _____

Thoughts, Emotions, and Behaviors

So far you've been practicing naming your emotions and figuring out their purpose. Next you need to know how thoughts, emotions, and behaviors are connected and how to tell them apart. Quite often we get these three things mixed up. For example, if someone asks you how you feel, and you respond, "I feel like people just don't understand me," this is actually describing not an emotion but a thought. We often mix up behaviors and emotions as well; you might think it's not good to get angry, but what you're probably thinking of is the behavior that often results from anger. It's okay to get angry, but it's not okay to yell at other people or throw things because you're angry. We tend to mix up how we feel, think, and act mainly because these three things are so closely connected.

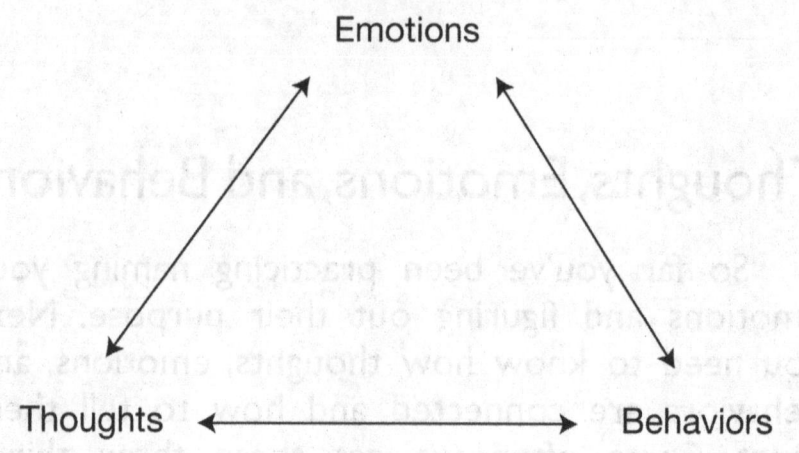

This diagram shows how our emotions affect our thoughts and behaviors, our thoughts affect our emotions and behaviors, and our behaviors affect our thoughts and emotions. In every situation, we experience these three things—we have thoughts about it, we have feelings about it, and we behave in a certain way. Add to this the fact that all three can happen very quickly, and it's no wonder we often get them confused! To be more effective at managing your emotions, you need to learn to separate these three things.

10 Thought, Emotion, or Behavior?

Read each sentence and indicate whether it's a thought, emotion, or behavior, by circling the most appropriate word. When you're done, you can check out the answers listed at the end of the book.

1. I really like school.   Thought   Emotion   Behavior

2. I'm worried about my ex- Thought   Emotion   Behavior
   ams next week.

3. I can't wait to get a new   Thought   Emotion   Behavior
   laptop.

4. I do my homework.   Thought   Emotion   Behavior

5. I argue with my parents.   Thought   Emotion   Behavior

6. I'm never going to have a Thought   Emotion   Behavior
   relationship.

7. I'm so angry I didn't get to Thought Emotion   Behavior
   go to the concert.

8. I surf the internet.   Thought   Emotion   Behavior

9. I love my new dog.   Thought   Emotion   Behavior

10. I get ready to go to the Thought   Emotion   Behavior
    mall with friends.

11. I don't like the sweater my Thought Emotion   Behavior
    grandmother bought me
    for my birthday.

12. I'm hurt that my sister   Thought   Emotion   Behavior
    wouldn't take me to the
    movies with her.

Don't worry if you had a hard time with some of these—most people aren't used to thinking this way. It's natural that it will take some time for you to get used to separating your thoughts from your emotions and your behaviors. Make sure you work on this, though, as it will help you be more able to manage your emotions and the behaviors that result from them.

11 Sorting Out Your Thoughts, Emotions, and Behaviors

Use the following worksheet to sort out your thoughts, emotions, and behaviors. You can also download the worksheet at http://www.newharbinger.com/47360. It's a great idea to fill in one of these worksheets whenever you're experiencing intense emotions or feeling confused about a situation; if you can't write about it during the situation, you can come back to complete the worksheet afterward. The sample entry here is based on Jacob's story from chapter 1.

Situation	Thought	Emotion	Behavior
I've been invited to a party at my friend's house, and most of my friends are going.	What if I get picked on again?	Anxiety, worry	I'm going to the party anyway.
	The last time I went to a party it was a disaster.	Shame, anger	While I was at the party, I tried to stay mindful and not think about the past.
	Part of me wants to go, but the other part of me wants to just say, "Forget it," and stay home.	Confusion, anxiety	

Situation	Thought	Emotion	Behavior
Describe in as much detail as possible the situation that triggered your thoughts, emotions, and behaviors. What was going on just before you started to think, feel, or behave this way?	What are your thoughts about the situation? These might include questions, memories, images, or judgments.	What emotions are you experiencing? If you can't figure out how you're feeling, start by remembering these four basic categories: *mad, sad, scared,* and *happy.*	What are you doing in the situation? This doesn't include urges or what you feel like doing; just describe what actions you are actually taking.

Thoughts and Feelings Are Not Facts

Just because you have a thought or an emotion doesn't mean it's true. You might think, *I'll never have a best friend,* but that's just a thought, not the truth. You might feel unloved, but that doesn't mean you actually *are* unloved—it's just how you feel. Our thoughts and feelings often *seem* true to us, so it's important to remember that they're just thoughts and feelings, not facts. This mindfulness exercise can help you practice noticing what's a thought, what's a feeling, and what's a behavior, and it will also help you just observe your thoughts and feelings and remember that they aren't facts.

12 Observing Your Thoughts and Emotions

Until you are familiar with this exercise, you might find it helpful to have someone read the instructions to you.

Observing your thoughts and emotions in a river

Sitting down in a relaxed position, close your eyes. In your mind, picture yourself standing in a shallow river. The water comes to just above your knees, and a gentle current pushes against your legs. As you stand in the river, notice your thoughts and emotions slowly start to float down the river, gliding past you on the current. Don't try to hold on to them as they float by, and don't get caught up in them; simply watch them as they float past you down the river. If you notice yourself getting caught up thinking about a thought or an emotion, so that you're going down the river with it instead of just watching it float past, come back to just standing in the river. Bring your attention back to the exercise and focus on just observing. As best you can, don't judge the thoughts or feelings that go by; just become aware of their presence.

Observing your thoughts and emotions in clouds

Here's a second way you can practice this exercise. Imagine yourself lying in a field of grass, looking up at fluffy white clouds. In each cloud, you can see a thought or a feeling you are experiencing; observe each thought or feeling as it slowly floats by. Don't judge them; just observe them as they float through your mind. As best as you can, don't try to grab the thoughts or emotions or get caught up thinking about them—just notice them. If you notice that you've gotten carried away with a particular cloud, bring yourself back to lying in the field of grass. If you notice your attention straying from the exercise, bring your attention back to observing the thoughts and emotions, without judging yourself.

Wrapping Up

In this chapter, you've practiced naming your emotions and learned that they serve a purpose. You've also learned that thoughts, emotions, and behaviors are interconnected and that it can be hard to separate them, but that doing so is very important in learning to manage your emotions more effectively. Finally, you learned to start thinking of your thoughts and emotions as just that—thoughts and emotions—rather than facts. As you go through this workbook, continue to practice the mindfulness exercises and other skills provided. It may take a lot of time and energy at the beginning, but the more you practice, the more effective you will become at not letting your emotions control you.

CHAPTER THREE

Taking Control of Out-of-Control Emotions

As you can see from what you've read so far, emotions are very complex. They're not just made up of how you *feel* but also include physical sensations, thoughts, urges, and behaviors. The information you learned about your emotions in chapter 2 will help you use the skills you'll learn in this chapter and the next to increase your ability to manage your emotions.

Three Different Ways of Thinking

We all have times when we're more controlled by our reasoning or logic, by our emotions, or by a combination of these two; these are the three different ways we think about things. Let's take a closer look at each.

Reasoning Self

The first of these three ways of thinking is what is known in DBT as *reasonable mind* (Linehan 1993). Basically, this refers to the self we use when we're thinking logically or factually about something. For example, when you're sitting in math class trying to work out a problem, you're probably using your reasoning self. On the first day of school, when you're trying to figure out where your locker is, you're probably using your reasoning self. When you're thinking from this perspective, there generally aren't very many emotions involved; any emotions you may be feeling tend to be fairly quiet ones, and they're really not influencing your behavior. See if you can come up with situations when you see things from this perspective and write them on the lines that follow. If you get stuck, ask someone you trust for help.

_____

_____

_____

Your reasoning self is very important, but thinking only from this perspective on a regular basis can lead to problems. For example, people who think from this perspective might regularly ignore how they feel, which can lead to difficulties managing emotions. Not being connected to your emotions can also make it difficult for you to understand and have empathy for others, which can cause problems in relationships.

Emotional Self

The opposite of the reasoning self is your emotional self, known in DBT as *emotion mind* (Linehan 1993). When you're thinking from your emotional self, your emotions are so intense that they control how you act; you *react* from the urges the emotions create in you, rather than *choosing how to act* in a situation. Here are some examples: you're feeling really angry and lash out at the people you care about; you're feeling depressed, so you hide away in your room and avoid talking to anyone; or you're feeling anxious about a party you were planning to go to, so you stay home instead.

Of course, you might also find yourself in your emotional self with pleasurable emotions. Think of a time when you felt love (or lust!) for someone, and these feelings controlled your behavior in some way: buying them a gift you couldn't really afford; sending way too many text messages or a photo of yourself, which maybe wasn't the best idea although it seemed like it at the time. Or think of a time when you got some fantastic news—you got into your first-choice college with a scholarship!—and you started calling all of your friends to share your excitement. This is also an example of the emotional self.

See if you can think of some examples of when you've acted from your emotional self, and write them on the lines that follow. Again, if you get stuck, ask someone you trust for help.

_____
_____
_____
_____

Just like with your reasoning self, if you're thinking from your emotional self and acting on these urges too often, you'll run into problems. As you can probably tell from the examples above, this is actually the self that most often gets us into trouble. So if we don't want to be acting from our reasoning or emotional selves all the time, what *do* we want to do? The answer is in the third way of thinking about things—using our wise self.

Wise Self

In order to get to your wise self—known in DBT as *wise mind* (Linehan 1993)—you need to combine your reasoning with your emotions so that neither mode of thinking is controlling you; instead, you're able to consider the consequences of your actions and subsequently act in your best interest and from your values. Have you ever found yourself in a situation that might have felt difficult, but you just knew what you had to do? Perhaps it wasn't the easiest thing to do, or what you really wanted to do in the situation, but it was what felt right, deep down? That's your wise self.

We all have this wisdom, and we all use it regularly, even though sometimes it might not feel like it. Here are some examples of acting from your wise self: you get angry with your parents about curfew, but you stop arguing, because you know they could say you can't go out at all; you're at a party and someone offers you drugs or alcohol, but you say no, because it goes against what you believe in; you have an urge to skip class but decide to go because you don't want to get too far behind. Can you think of some times when you've acted from this perspective? Write them here, asking someone you trust for help if you need it.

_____
_____
_____
_____

It can be helpful to have a *shortcut* to each of these states—people who represent these different thinking perspectives for you—a reasoning person, an emotional person, and a wise person. Then, when you find yourself struggling with a difficult situation, you can bring them to mind to help you figure out what perspective you're thinking from and get to a more balanced perspective. For example, you could ask yourself, *What would Mom do?* if she is represents that internal wisdom. Consider who might represent these different perspectives for you. You might think of an actor, a sports star, a political or religious figure, or it could be someone in your own life, such as a family member, a friend, a mentor, or a pastor, coach, or teacher. Fill in the blanks with your answers.

Reasoning: _____
Emotional: _____
Wise: _____

13 Reasoning, Emotional, or Wise Self?

For each of the following stories, see if you can determine which way of thinking is being depicted—reasoning self, emotional self, or wise self—and circle the one that is most appropriate. A list of answers is provided at the end of the book.

1. Tanya was at a party when a friend passed her a bottle of beer. She thought, *Everyone else is drinking. Will they accept me if I don't?* Then she remembered that she had an important exam on Monday; she realized she wouldn't study well the next day if she got drunk that night, so she said, "No thanks."

Reasoning Self   Emotional Self   Wise Self

2. Ty was really nervous about asking Jessica to the prom, but he got up his courage and asked her anyway. When she turned him down, he was devastated at first, but then he thought to himself, *Whatever—it's better this way because I can really only afford to buy one ticket.*

Reasoning Self   Emotional Self   Wise Self

3. Makenna was so angry at her parents because they wouldn't let her go camping with her friends this weekend. She asked them again near the end of the week, but they weren't budging on their decision. She was so disappointed and frustrated that she started to yell at her parents and told them she hated them.

Reasoning Self   Emotional Self   Wise Self

4. Riley often worried about fitting in with the other kids at school, which made it hard for him to socialize. One day he decided enough was enough—he was just going to start doing it anyway. He knew he always had a good time when he did spend time with friends, so he approached a group of

people at school and joined in the conversation, even though he felt anxious.

Reasoning Self   Emotional Self   Wise Self

5. Catrina was taking an English exam. Even though she felt it was going fairly well, she decided to throw in some extra facts, like Shakespeare's date and place of birth, which she figured might score her some additional marks.

Reasoning Self   Emotional Self   Wise Self

6. Jody was playing around on his skateboard at school when he noticed a bunch of kids watching him. He wanted to impress them, so he decided to try a really hard trick on the stairs to make himself look good, even though he wasn't sure he'd be able to land it.

Reasoning Self   Emotional Self   Wise Self

14 Your Typical Way of Thinking

Now that you have a better understanding of these three different ways of thinking about things, it's important to start using these skills in your own life. The first step is to assess your patterns in the present. You may find that you act from more than one of these perspectives, depending on the situation and the people you're dealing with. Put a check mark beside the statements that you think apply to you most often, to help you determine if you tend to think more from one of these perspectives than the others.

Am I a reasoner?

☐ I often ignore my emotions when making a decision.

☐ I usually have logical reasons for the things I do.

☐ I am often unaware of what emotions I'm feeling.

☐ I am more comfortable talking about facts than feelings.

Am I ruled by my emotions?

☐ I frequently act on urges, for example, saying or doing things I later regret.

☐ I regularly find myself in crisis situations, where my emotions are really intense and I have a hard time thinking straight.

☐ I often make decisions based solely on how I feel about a situation.

☐ I tend to question decisions after I've made them, worrying about whether or not it was the right choice.

Do I tend to be wise?

☐ I usually take into account both logic and emotions when making a decision.

☐ I often feel calm and at peace after making a decision which I've sat with for a while.

☐ I am mostly comfortable allowing myself to feel my emotions.

☐ I often act in ways that move me toward my long-term goals.

Now add up your check marks for each category and see if you fall predominantly into one or another—you may or you may not.

It's very important to start being more aware of what thinking style you're using, as this will help you make effective changes in your life. Over the coming days, try to be more mindful of what perspective you're thinking from: reasoning self, emotional self, or wise self. This mindfulness exercise is simply about increasing your awareness, so you don't have to write anything down, but it is important, because you can't do anything to change your thinking style until you realize which one you've been using.

If you have trouble remembering to do this check-in, think of some ways to help yourself remember: put sticky notes up on your dresser or on your bathroom mirror; write notes to yourself in your journal or agenda; make a sign that you can put on the fridge or in your locker at school; put a daily recurring appointment in your cell phone that will remind you. Do whatever you need to do to remind yourself to ask the question: *Am I thinking from my reasoning self, from my emotional self, or from my wise self?*

In addition to increasing your awareness, of course, it's important to practice! How do you practice increasing your wisdom? Here are some activities to try. Choose one that fits best for you—or feel free to make up your own!—and practice it regularly in everyday situations, outside of anything problematic. This will make it more likely that you'll be able to access that wise part of yourself when problems do arise and emotions become more intense.

1. Ask yourself, *What does my wise self tell me?* Or imagine the person who represents your wise person and ask yourself, *What would my wise person do or say in this situation?* Then listen quietly and see if you get an answer. You might find it helpful to close your eyes as you do this.
2. Practice a breathing exercise to get to your wise self. Here's one to help you get to that balanced place: As you inhale slowly and deeply, say to yourself the words *Get to* ... And as you slowly exhale, add the words *my wise self.* Keep doing this for a couple of minutes. Notice when your mind wanders from your breathing and this mantra, accept it, and bring your attention back. You can change these words if others would fit better for you.
3. Using your imagination, practice getting to your wise self by turning inward and going

to a place that in some way resonates for you. Many people feel they have a wise place inside of them, sometimes near their heart, sometimes in the area that our deep breaths come from. You can create a picture in your mind of your own wise, knowing place and imagine yourself turning inward and going there.

Remember, this should feel comfortable for you, so experiment with these and other practices that you might make up yourself. If this is hard for you at the beginning, and you're not sure if you're getting to your wise self, you might also want to ask someone (like your wise person) for their opinion on whether you're acting from your reasoning, emotional, or wise self.

Your Physical Health Can Affect Your Thinking Style

Believe it or not, the way you treat yourself physically can influence the extent to which you find yourself stuck in your emotional self, being controlled by your emotions (Linehan 1993). Read the following stories, which demonstrate how various aspects of your physical health can make it harder for you to manage your emotions. Then answer the questions in activity 15 to help you evaluate which of these areas you need to work on.

Sleep

Anthony had been having problems with his mood since eleventh grade. He would sometimes feel pretty low, and he got anxious a lot, especially in social situations. In his final year of high school, the pressure seemed to really get to him. He would come home from school and sleep until dinnertime, watch TV or play video games after dinner, and then go back to bed. It felt like he was constantly tired and just couldn't get enough sleep. On weekends, he would get up late in the morning, or even early in the afternoon, and would try to get some schoolwork done, but he just felt too exhausted to concentrate and would end up going back to bed.

Jonathan also struggled with his emotions, often feeling angry and sad. Unlike Anthony, though, Jonathan didn't sleep enough. He was quite disciplined in his schoolwork, getting home after school or hockey practice on a weeknight and going straight to his room to study until dinnertime. After dinner, he'd do some more work and then take some time for himself—he'd play video games, chat online with friends, or just watch TV. He would often stay up until after midnight and would be up again at seven the next morning to get ready for school. Jonathan was constantly tired, but he ignored his fatigue, because there was so much he had to get done; what he didn't recognize was lack of sleep was running him down emotionally as well.

Both Anthony and Jonathan are having problems balancing their sleep. Too much sleep or too little sleep can increase the amount of time you spend in your emotional self and affect your ability to manage your emotions.

Eating

Brianna knew she had a problem with eating. Sometimes she could go for days without eating much of anything; at other times she found herself eating large quantities of food and feeling out of control. When she wasn't eating much, Brianna noticed that she felt very tired, had no energy, and was more likely to snap at people for little things. When she was overeating, she'd get really down on herself and end up feeling quite depressed.

Balancing your eating habits is also very helpful in improving your ability to manage emotions. As Brianna found, eating too much or too little usually leads you to act more often from your emotional self.

Treating Physical Illness

Justin was diagnosed with diabetes when he was fourteen. He had a hard time accepting this diagnosis, because he felt it made him different. It was also inconvenient; he was supposed to check his blood four times a day and give himself insulin shots regularly. It was difficult to find time to do the things he needed to do to treat his diabetes, especially because he didn't want his friends to know about it and so he tried to keep it hidden. That meant that he would often miss checking his blood, and sometimes he'd even miss doses of his insulin. Justin had been told that this wasn't safe and that it could lead to serious health problems; he did notice that he would sometimes get light-headed, have a hard time concentrating, and be short-tempered, but Justin just wanted to be like everyone else.

Many people develop health problems, such as diabetes or asthma, at a young age. Sometimes people have injuries that cause chronic pain or other problems that need to be treated as well. If you have any kind of physical illness or pain, it's extremely important that you treat it the way your doctor tells you to. Not doing this can cause further health problems for you, and it can also result in more emotions for you, the way Justin became more irritable when he didn't take his insulin. Managing any physical health problems you have will also help you manage your emotions.

> ## Exercise
>
> Luisa was diagnosed with depression and anxiety when she was fifteen. Her doctor had suggested that she first try making some changes in her lifestyle rather than taking medicine to help with these problems. One of the changes that Luisa's doctor emphasized was for her to get more exercise. The doctor told Luisa that exercise is actually a natural antidepressant, producing brain chemicals that help us feel good. Luisa wasn't big into exercise, but she decided she'd rather avoid taking medication if she could, so she gave it a try. She began by going for walks three times a week, for about fifteen minutes each time, and gradually worked her way up to forty-five-minute walks four to six times a week. Luisa found that this exercise did help her feel better and that she actually enjoyed the walks and the break they gave her from being in the house doing homework or chores.

Exercise can't always take the place of medication, but it certainly helps you feel better. We all know that exercise is good for us physically, but as Luisa found, exercise can also improve your mood and decrease anxiety. For people with anger problems, exercise is also a great outlet, and, in general, it will increase your ability to manage your emotions in healthier ways.

> ## Drugs and Alcohol
>
> Ramjeet started drinking at parties with his friends when he was about seventeen. He didn't think it was a big deal—alcohol was legal, even if he was under the legal drinking age. Everybody drank—his parents, his older brother—and Ramjeet was responsible when he drank, always making sure he had a ride home. What Ramjeet began to notice, however, was that every time he drank, he would experience being moodier for a few days afterward—one minute he was fine, the next minute he'd be snapping at someone for something fairly small. Ramjeet decided to stop drinking to see if this made a difference in his mood, and he found that he was much less irritable when he wasn't drinking.

Drugs and alcohol are known as mood-altering substances, and if you use them, you have no control over how your emotional state is altered; you might notice that your experience varies from time to time, that it's often not the same as the time before. You might also notice that, while you're using, you tend to act on your urges more often, and you'll be more likely to make decisions that aren't so wise—like maybe driving while you're high or drunk or getting into other dangerous situations. As Ramjeet realized, stopping the use of these kinds of substances increases your ability to manage yourself and your emotions.

15 Lifestyle Changes You Can Make to Decrease Emotions

Certain things you do in your daily life may be increasing the amount of time you're spending in your emotional self. Answer the following questions to determine which area or areas you need to work on. Take your time as you think about what kinds of changes you can start working on right away to increase your ability to manage emotions.

Sleep

Approximately how many hours of sleep do you get each night? ____

Do you generally feel rested when you wake up? ____

Do you usually take a nap in the afternoon? If so, for how long? ____

After you nap, do you usually feel better or worse? ____

Do you ingest substances that could be interfering with your ability to get good sleep, such as caffeine or other stimulants (think coffee, tea, energy drinks, caffeine pills, diet pills)? ____

Do you use your phone or another device right up until bedtime? ____

Based on your answers above, and keeping in mind that too much or too little sleep usually leaves you feeling lethargic and sluggish, do you think you need to increase or decrease the amount of time you're sleeping? _____

If you have identified this as an area to work on, what is one small step you can take to start working toward that goal? (For example, if you need to increase your sleep, you could set a goal to go to bed a half hour earlier tonight, then work your way up to an hour; or you might identify that you need to reduce or eliminate caffeine to help you sleep better. Keep in mind that technology should also be turned off at least thirty minutes before bedtime to contribute to better sleep.) _____

Eating

Do you eat three meals as well as some snacks each day? _____

Do your meals and snacks tend to be healthy? _____

Do you find yourself eating just because you have an urge to—maybe out of boredom or because you're feeling a painful emotion, such as sadness? _____

Do you find yourself not eating so you can lose weight or feel more in control? _____

Sometimes people develop problems with eating for which they need to seek professional help. If you feel you have an eating problem and are unable to manage it on your own, please speak to someone you trust. If this is not the case, but you have identified eating as an area to work on, what is one small step you can take to start working toward that goal? (For example, if you currently eat only one meal a day, you could set a goal to begin eating something small for breakfast and work your way up.) _____

Treating physical illness

Do you have a physical illness that requires medication or some other kind of treatment, such as physiotherapy? If so, do you take your medication or follow your doctor's directions for treatment?

If you have identified this as an area to work on, what is one small step you can take to start working toward that goal? (For example, you could learn more about your illness to understand why the medication or treatment is necessary.)

Exercise

Do you currently do any type of exercise? If so, how often and for how long?

Keep in mind that if you have any kind of health problems, you'll want to check with your doctor before you start an exercise routine. If you have identified exercise as an area to work on, what is one small step you can take to start working toward that goal? (For example, if you currently exercise once or twice a week for fifteen minutes, you could increase this to three times a week and work your way up to more.)

Drugs and alcohol

Do you currently drink alcohol or use street drugs? If so, how often? (If you're nervous about writing this information down here, you can do it on a separate piece of paper or simply think about it.)

Do you see this use causing problems for you in school, work, relationships, or any other aspect of your life?

Has anyone else in your life ever told you that your drinking ____
or drug use is a problem?

When you're using drugs or alcohol, do you tend to make ____
poor decisions or behave in ways that you later regret?

Do you find yourself turning to drugs or alcohol to deal with ____
your emotions?

If you have identified this as an area to work on, what is one ____
small step you can take to start working toward that goal?
(For example, if alcohol is a problem, you could set a goal to
drink only one night on the weekend instead of two and decrease your consumption from there. If you don't think this
is a problem you can handle on your own, you might set a
goal to look into AA groups for teens or ask someone you
trust for help.)

Being Effective

This section and the next will focus on some skills that can help you move toward your long-term goals.

Our goals can easily get lost when we act from our emotional self: acting on an urge, doing what *feels good* rather than what's going to be more helpful or healthy for us in the long run. For example, you feel like your math teacher isn't treating you fairly and is giving you lower grades than you deserve. One day you get so angry that you talk back, saying hurtful things to your teacher to get back at her for the anger she's caused, and you storm out of the room. This might feel good at the time, but what do you think the end result will be? Chances are you'll get detention or some other kind of punishment for being disrespectful, and your teacher isn't very likely to look kindlier on you when she's marking your tests in the future. This is an example of being *ineffective*—your behavior (acting on your urge) might have been satisfying in the short term, and it might have felt good to yell at your teacher, but it also made it harder for you to reach your long-term goals.

Can you think of times when you've been ineffective? Write down a couple of situations here:

_____

_____

_____

Now that you can relate to what it means to be ineffective, let's look at how you could be more effective. The DBT skill of being *effective* is about acting from your wise self—not acting on your urge or just doing what feels good but, instead, assessing what you can do to move closer to your long-term goals or doing what you need to do to get your needs met (Linehan 1993).

To be effective, you first have to figure out what your goals are. Once you determine what your long-term goal is in a situation, you need to consider what you could do that might move you closer to your goal. Keep in mind that acting effectively doesn't guarantee that you'll get what you're after in a situation. If you're acting skillfully, of course, your chances of getting what you want will improve, but skills don't come with guarantees! Let's look at an example to help you understand the skill of being effective.

Kyle's Story

Kyle had a plan. He was going to college on a baseball scholarship, and he was going to become a doctor and would be able to financially support his mother, who had done so much for him since his dad had taken off years ago. This had been the plan since he was fourteen. He was now seventeen and things were on track—his grades were good, and he was being scouted for some top schools. But Kyle was under a lot of pressure. If he didn't get a scholarship, there was no way his mom would be able to afford to send him to school, even though she had been working two jobs for years trying to save money for his education.

One day in baseball practice, the coach was riding Kyle hard, and Kyle snapped. He started to yell back and almost came to blows with the coach, which ended up getting him suspended from practice. He was told he couldn't return until he had taken some anger-management classes. Kyle thought this was ridiculous: he didn't have anger problems; it was the coach's fault for getting on him too

> much. However, Kyle knew he was so close to receiving a scholarship, and this could blow his chances. He agreed to the classes even though he didn't think they were necessary, and he was allowed back to practice before it was too late.

So what do you think of Kyle's story? Maybe you think it wasn't fair or that Kyle shouldn't have given in. Well, Kyle was effective. It probably would have felt much better for Kyle to tell the coach off and refuse the anger-management classes, but he recognized that doing so would not get him closer to his long-term goal and would actually harm his chances of reaching that goal. So Kyle did what he had to do to keep moving toward his goal.

One thing that often gets in the way of being effective is our thoughts about a situation. Quite often we react to how we think a situation *should* be rather than to how it really *is*. Looking at the earlier example, maybe you think that your math teacher hasn't been treating you fairly, so why shouldn't you tell her how you really feel? Here's another example: your parents have set your nightly curfew for nine o'clock, but it's the weekend, and you're with a friend your parents know well, so you think, *This is silly. I don't need to be home by nine.* You stay out later, only to be grounded by your parents when you come home past curfew. These are examples of how we respond not to the reality of the situation itself but to how we think the situation should be (Linehan 1993).

So, to be effective in a situation, you have to use your wise self. It makes sense that you would be angry if you were being treated unfairly by a teacher, but rather than letting this anger control your actions so that you yell at your teacher and walk out the door, you need to bring in your other thinking styles. Your reasoning self, for example, might have you think about the fact that if you get detention after school, you won't be able to go try out for the school play. This will help you get to your wise self, figure out what your goal is, and think of what you can do to act in your own best interest; for example, you might think, *I'm angry with how I've been treated by my math teacher, but I don't want to get a detention, and I want her to be more willing to give me the grades I think I deserve in the future.*

16 How to Be More Effective

Now it's your turn to think about ways you could be more effective. Think of a current, past, or future situation in which you could practice being effective. Consider the questions below to figure out what you can do (or what you could have done differently) to help you get your needs met in this situation.

88

Describe the situation: _____
_____
_____

What are your thoughts and emotions about this situation? _____
_____

What is your emotional self telling you to do in this situation? In other words, what would you like to do that might feel good but would probably be ineffective?
_____
_____

What long-term goal or goals do you have in this situation? _____
_____

What would be an effective thing to do in this situation? In other words, what can you do to increase your chances of meeting your long-term goal(s)?

If you have a hard time with this exercise, try asking yourself what you would tell a friend who was in a similar situation or what your wise person might do. You can also ask someone you trust for help.

Acting Opposite to Your Urge

Now let's look at another skill that can help you manage your emotions more effectively: *acting opposite to your urge*. This means doing the opposite of what your emotional self tells you to do when you're experiencing a strong emotion. For example, when you feel angry, your urge may be to attack, verbally or physically. When you feel sad or depressed, your urge may be to isolate yourself or to hide away from others. And when you feel anxious or afraid, it's likely that you'll want to avoid or escape from whatever is causing the fear. Quite often, you go along with urges like these because you're thinking from your emotional self and it feels like the right thing to do. But if you were to stop and look at the situation from your wise self, you would see that acting on these urges is usually not in your best interest. In fact, doing so usually just intensifies the emotion you're experiencing. For example, if you verbally attack the person you're angry with, you're actually fueling your anger and likely not acting in a way that's consistent with your values, which can trigger negative thoughts and painful feelings toward yourself later on (Van Dijk 2009). Likewise, if you hide away from others when you're feeling sad, you end up feeling more alone and disconnected, which intensifies your sadness. And avoiding situations that cause you anxiety ends up increasing your anxiety in the long run as well as triggering other emotions like sadness and frustration because you can't do the things you'd like to do.

Acting opposite to your urge has you do exactly what it sounds like—first you identify the urge that's attached to your emotion, and then you do the opposite. But acting opposite to your urge is a skill that's used only when an emotion isn't justified, or when it's not effective for you to continue feeling that emotion. As we discussed earlier, emotions serve a purpose. If you identify that you *should* be feeling afraid right now, because there's a car speeding toward you as you're crossing the road, please do what the fear is telling you to do—run to keep yourself safe! But when an emotion has already come and delivered its message—in other words, you know how you feel about a situation and you're ready to do something about it—then strong emotions can get in the way of your being able to act effectively. When an emotion remains intense, it's hard to get to your wise self and to act in healthy, helpful ways for yourself. For example, if you're feeling really angry with someone, the intensity of the anger can make it difficult to have a productive conversation with that person. Or, if you're feeling anxious about going to a party, the intensity of your anxiety can get in the way of your meeting new people and having a good time. So the thing to keep in mind with this skill is that if the emotion you're experiencing *isn't* justified by the situation, or is no longer helpful and you want to reduce it, then act opposite to your urge. Look at the following chart to see what acting opposite means for different emotions.

Emotion	When Is It Justified?	Urge	How to Act Opposite
Anger	When there's something getting in our way, blocking us from reaching a goal	Lash out, attack someone or something, physically or verbally.	Be respectful or civil; if this feels too difficult, gently avoid the person or the situation.
	When we or someone we care about is begin attacked, threatened, insulted, or hurt by others	Judge the person or situation with whom or with which you're angry.	Change judgments to nonjudgmental, accepting thoughts.
Sadness	When things aren't the way we expected them to be or when we've experienced a loss of some sort	Hide away from others, disconnect; isolate yourself.	Reach out and connect with others.
		Stop doing your regular activities.	Reengage in your usual activities.
Fear or Anxiety	When there is a threat to our safety or our well-being or to that of someone we care about	Avoid whatever is causing the fear or anxiety.	Approach the situation or person causing the fear or anxiety.
		Escape or leave the situation causing fear or anxiety.	Stay in the situation.
Guilt	When we've done something that goes against our values	Stop the behavior causing guilt; make repair (apologize).	Continue the behavior; don't apologize or try to make repair in other ways.

Emotion	When Is It Justified?	Urge	How to Act Opposite
Shame	When we've done something that will cause us to be rejected by people in our lives we care about	Hide away from others, disconnect and isolate yourself.	Reach out to others who you feel confident will accept and support you; connect; share what you're feeling shame about.
	When there is something about us (a personal characteristic) that would cause others to reject us if they found out	Judge yourself.	Change self-judgments to nonjudgments; radically accept; self-validate.
Love	When we love someone or something who does things or has qualities that we value or admire	Seek connection with the person you love; reach out.	Avoid connection with the person you love; don't act on the urge to reach out.
	When our love enhances the quality of our life (or that of those we care about)		
	When our love increases our chances of attaining our own personal goals		

Think back to Kyle's example. He was angry that he had to take anger-management classes. If that intense anger had just stuck around, it would have made it difficult for Kyle to make a wise decision and act in an effective way. Acting opposite to your urge helps decrease the intensity of the emotion so that you can get to your wise mind and act in ways that will be more effective for you.

One thing you need to know about using this skill with anger and shame is that these emotions don't come with just a behavioral urge—in other words, they don't affect just your actions. These emotions also affect your thoughts about a situation or a person, usually in the form of judgments (Linehan 1993). So, if you're trying to act opposite to your urge with anger or shame, you need to both *act* and *think* opposite, or think in a nonjudgmental way. We'll be looking more at this skill in the next chapter—for now, just remember that anger and shame show up not only in your behavior but also in your thoughts.

About Guilt and Shame

In chapter 2 you learned about some of the more painful emotions we experience, including guilt and shame. Guilt and shame often feel very similar; they frequently come up together, so it's easy to confuse them. But they are quite different, and it's important to learn to tell the difference: Remember that guilt is the emotion we are justified in feeling when we've done something that goes against our values; it stops us from doing that behavior (or from continuing to do it), and it causes us to try to repair the harm we've done.

Shame, on the other hand, is justified when we've done something, or when there's something about us as a person, that could cause us to be rejected by others if they found out. Shame is the feeling that protects us by keeping us quiet about a behavior or personal characteristic, to keep us connected to people who are important to us. The problem is that many of us experience these emotions even when we haven't done anything to feel guilty or ashamed about. Does that ever happen to you?

Many people feel guilty when they're not doing anything they consider productive—in other words, when they're doing things that are relaxing or they're just taking time to care for themselves. Some people feel guilty for thinking certain things or experiencing certain emotions—or even for the dreams they have at night! None of these are behaviors to feel guilty about. If you take something that doesn't belong to you or treat someone in a hurtful or disrespectful way, then yes, feeling guilty is justified. Remember, this emotion tells us we've acted in a way that our conscience disapproves of. If this is the case, then you need to stop the behavior and perhaps make amends. But if you haven't acted in a way that goes against your values, continuing to engage in that behavior will cause the guilt to gradually dissipate.

Feeling shame is justified if we've taken something that doesn't belong to us; if we've hurt someone on purpose; or if we've done something that goes against societal norms like drinking and driving – shame is such a strong, uncomfortable feeling that it typically stops us from doing these things (and that's also a function that this emotion provides). But shame is a little more complicated than that. Take this example: Liz had grown up knowing she was attracted to other girls, not guys. When she started high school, someone started telling everyone she was gay, even though she hadn't told even her closest friends. It felt like she had to keep this a secret, because she knew that others in her small, religious town often didn't accept people who were "different." When people started saying she was gay, Liz felt ashamed, and she denied it. Even though she was comfortable with her own sexuality, she knew that others would likely not accept it, and so she wanted to keep it hidden.

In this situation, shame protected Liz by having her keep her secret, which allowed her to stay connected to the people who were important to her but who may have rejected her had they known the truth. By the way, if Liz had known that those friends would *not* have rejected her, the shame would not have been justified, and we would want Liz to share her truth with her friends. Or, if she had decided to find a community where she would be accepted (for example, an LGBTQI+ group), where she could be certain of not being rejected, shame would not be justified. Connection is what helps us to reduce shame, whereas staying silent and keeping something a secret is what makes it grow stronger (Brown 2012).

Self-judgment also contributes to feelings of shame. If Liz was judging herself as *defective, worthless,* or *weird,* for example, this would have increased the painful feeling of shame as well, further preventing her from thinking that she could connect with others and share her secret. So the other part to reducing feelings of shame is to practice being nonjudgmental toward yourself. Again, with guilt and shame, if you've done something that goes against your values, stop the behavior and make amends if you need to. But if your behavior isn't something you should feel guilty about or ashamed of, the painful feelings will slowly decrease over time if you continue to engage in the behavior and if you connect with others around this behavior or this characteristic of yourself.

Sometimes people think that acting opposite to their urge means they have to stuff their emotions or pretend they're not experiencing them; for example, with anger, they should pretend they're not angry and be nice to the other person. This is not the case! Stuffing your emotions is never effective—it makes things worse, and it makes it harder for you to manage your emotions. Acting opposite to your urge is a skill that's only used when it's not helpful for you to continue to feel an intense emotion. In other words, the emotion has come up, you acknowledge it and understand why it's there, and now it's getting in the way of your ability to get to your wise self and act effectively.

Let's sum up this skill with a quick review:

How to Act Opposite

Step 1. Figure out what the emotion is that you're experiencing; validate the emotion by just acknowledging or accepting it (we'll look at this in more detail in chapter 5).

Step 2. Figure out what the emotion is telling you to do—what's the urge?

Step 3. Ask yourself if the emotion is justified by the situation; if it's not, go to step 4. If it is justified, ask yourself if acting on the urge is going to be effective—if it is, don't act opposite to the urge, but do what it's telling you to do.

Step 4: Ask yourself if you want to change the emotion. If you do, figure out what the opposite action is, and go to step 5.

Step 5: Do the opposite of the urge, and repeat it until the emotion goes down.

17 Acting Opposite to Urges

This exercise can help you analyze situations in which you have acted opposite to your urge as well as times when you've been unable to do this. Thinking about when you've been able to act skillfully as well as when you haven't can help you see what is—and isn't—working and what you could do next time to be more effective. Fill in the emotion you were experiencing and the urge that was attached to it. If you acted on the urge, follow the *yes* path, answering the questions to help you assess the outcome. Likewise, if you didn't act on the urge, follow the *no* path. You can also download this worksheet at http://www.newharbinger.com/47360 for future use.

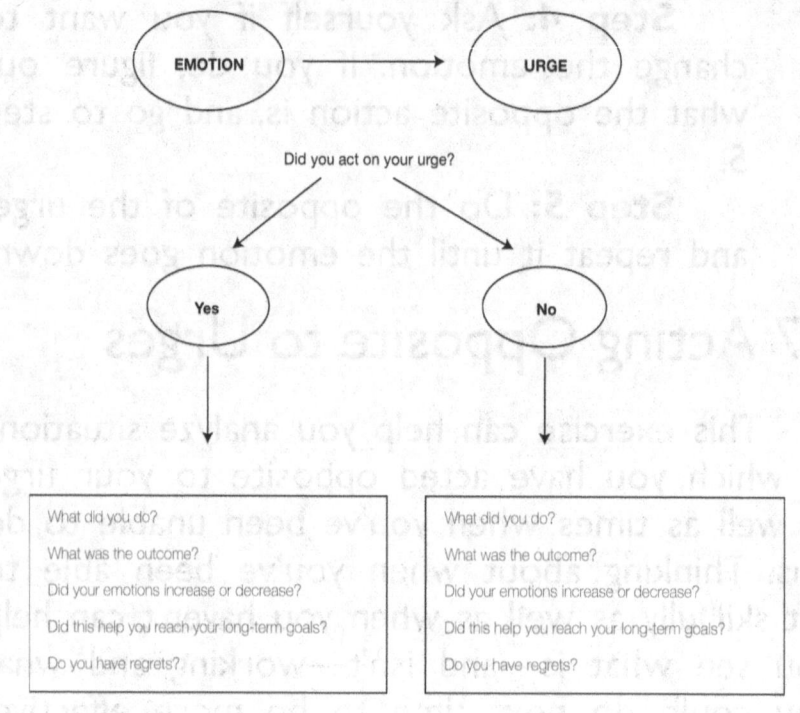

Wrapping Up

In this chapter, you learned about the three different ways that we think about things—with our reasoning self, our emotional self, and our wise self. Then you learned about some changes you can make in your life that will make you less vulnerable to being controlled by your emotional self. You also looked at two skills to help you act in ways that will make it more likely for you to reach your goals. Before moving on, make sure you're really working on incorporating these changes into your life and practicing these skills to reduce the control your emotions have over you.

CHAPTER FOUR

Reducing Your Painful Emotions

Hopefully you've been working on making some changes in your life to be less controlled by your emotions. Even with these changes, you'll find that you still have times when your emotions get really intense, making it hard to manage them. In this chapter, we'll be looking at three related skills—reducing judgments, accepting your emotions, and accepting reality—that can help you reduce the intensity of the emotional pain you experience.

Reducing Judgments

Have you ever noticed that when you're angry, frustrated, hurt, or feeling other painful emotions, you have a tendency to judge whoever (or whatever) is triggering these painful emotions for you? For example, if a close friend tells someone your secret, you may think about how "mean" that person is. Perhaps when you get a low grade on a paper you worked really hard on, in your mind you call your teacher a name. Or maybe in this same scenario, you don't judge your teacher but judge yourself, thinking about how "stupid" you are.

What Does Being Nonjudgmental Mean?

When we judge things, we use shorthand labels that don't really provide helpful information. Then we often think about these judgments as though they were facts when they're really not—they're judgments. For example, calling your close friend "mean" is a label that doesn't explain why you think he's mean or provide any information about the situation you're referring to. If you told another friend you thought your friend was mean, without providing the rest of the story, he wouldn't know what you meant.

In contrast, you can think of being nonjudgmental as talking about facts and feelings. Instead of calling your friend "mean," you might say something like "He betrayed my confidence, and I'm hurt and angered by his actions." If you were to say that to another friend, he would understand what you meant.

To help clarify this, let's look at the example of calling your teacher a name. When you get a low grade on a paper you worked really hard on, you tell yourself your teacher is a *jerk*. This is a judgment, a label you've stuck on your teacher that doesn't really explain anything. Instead of using this label, try thinking about what you might really mean by this. To be nonjudgmental, you might think instead, *I'm so angry at my teacher for giving me this grade. I worked really hard on that paper, and I believe I deserve more than a C+.* Get the difference? You're being clear and specific, and you're stating the facts of the situation and your feelings about it.

As you continue to read, keep in mind that this is a really tough skill to learn, so make sure you practice the exercises here, and you will get it! The following activity will help you start to understand the difference between judgments and nonjudgments.

18 Judgments vs. Nonjudgments

Read each of the following statements. Decide whether the statement is judgmental or nonjudgmental, and circle the word to indicate this; a list of answers appears at the end of the book.

1. I should have gotten higher marks on my report card.   Judgment   Nonjudgment

2. My parents can be so mean sometimes.   Judgment   Nonjudgment

3. I'm a loser.   Judgment   Nonjudgment

4. I get so frustrated with myself when I lose control of my anger.   Judgment   Nonjudgment

5. My brother really annoys me when he won't get off the computer and I need it. Judgment Nonjudgment

6. R & B music is the best. Judgment Nonjudgment

7. I'm really enjoying my math class this year, but I still find it hard. Judgment Nonjudgment

8. I don't think it's safe to post pictures of myself on Instagram. Judgment Nonjudgment

9. I'm really disappointed that I wasn't invited to prom. Judgment Nonjudgment

You might have noticed from these examples that judgments can be negative or positive. For the purpose of managing your emotions, we're more concerned with the negative judgments, since they're the ones that cause more emotional pain. However, it's helpful to practice being aware of when you're making positive or negative judgments.

Don't "Should" Yourself

You may have heard this saying before: "Don't *should* yourself." This is often a helpful guideline, since the words *should* and *shouldn't* often fall into the judgmental category, but it's also not quite so black and white. It will be helpful to take a closer look.

Take an example from the previous exercise: "I should have gotten higher marks on my report card." Hopefully, you recognized that this is a judgmental statement, because the word *should* in this statement is judgmental. When we use this word, there's often another piece that's implied but unspoken, such as, *There's something wrong with me because I didn't get higher marks* or *Therefore I'm a bad student.* Likewise, with the word *shouldn't*: "I shouldn't have said that to my friend" leads us to assume a judgment, like *I'm bad that I said that to my friend.*

You can check this out yourself: think of a recent time when you told yourself that you should or shouldn't have done something. (You might recall, *I should have gotten more homework done today* or *I shouldn't have gotten into a fight with my sister.*) Remember how you felt when you told yourself this. What emotions showed up? Did you feel guilt, shame, anger, or disappointment in yourself? Now notice how this felt in your body: did you feel tension somewhere? Perhaps your posture became more slouched or hunched? Maybe you felt a weight on your shoulders, a tightness in your chest, or an urge to cry? And, of course, maybe you didn't notice any of these things, and that's okay as well. Just try to recall what happened. Now what about your thoughts? Did you have follow-up judgments at the time, like *What's wrong with me that I have no motivation to work?* or *Why am I such a bad sister?* If you noticed any of these things, you can be pretty sure that your *should* or *shouldn't* was, in fact, a judgment.

If you didn't notice any of these things, it could very well be that you used this word in a nonjudgmental way. For example, just adding the words *in order to* after the word *should* or *shouldn't* turns what's being said into a factual statement. Going back to the earlier example, "I should have gotten higher marks on my report card" is a judgment. But when you say instead, "I should have gotten higher marks on my report card in order to get into the college I wanted," the judgment disappears. You're giving a factual reason for why you should have or should not have done something—and there's no hidden judgment behind the statement—which means you're not adding fuel to the fire.

Who knew this was going to be so complicated, right?

The Importance of Being Nonjudgmental

Unfortunately, judgments are common in our society. We hear them all the time, and so we get into the habit of thinking or saying them often as well. The thing is, judgments are unhelpful. They don't make us feel better, and quite often they actually increase the amount of pain we're experiencing. Think of your emotion as a fire and the judgments as fuel—every time you judge, out loud or just in your thoughts, you're adding fuel to the fire of your emotion.

19 Adding Fuel to the Fire

Think of a time when you've been really angry—with yourself or someone else—and see if you can identify the judgments you were thinking or saying that added fuel to your anger. Write them in the spaces that follow. If you can't think of a situation that you remember well enough, you can come back to this exercise when you have a more recent situation to use.

Judgments are often difficult to catch, because we judge so automatically. What did you notice while you were doing this exercise? For example, did you have a hard time figuring out what was a judgment and what wasn't? Maybe you noticed that just thinking about this situation again brought back the emotions about it. Write your observations here:

Sometimes Judgments Are Necessary

So far, I've been talking about the fact that judging tends to create more pain for us. But, in fact, judgments are sometimes necessary. If you're about to cross the road, for instance, and the red hand starts flashing, you have to decide whether to continue walking. This is you making a judgment: safe or not safe? This type of judgment is necessary, and it isn't going to trigger pain for you. Similarly, if you've ever gone grocery shopping with your parents, you'll notice that they make judgments about what produce is "good" or "bad;" they make these judgment calls, and these aren't judgments that will trigger painful emotions. To help distinguish between these necessary judgments and the judgments that are unnecessary and problematic, I'm going to refer to necessary judgments as *evaluations*.

You have to be evaluated in school to determine how you're doing and whether you're ready to move on—this is a necessary judgment. At times people also learn by evaluating themselves; for example, you have to evaluate your own behavior in a situation to determine if you've acted appropriately or if perhaps you made a mistake and need to apologize or correct your behavior in another way. But keep in mind, that even if you've made a mistake and regret something you said or did, you still need to talk to yourself about it in a kind way. If you had an argument with your mom and said something you regret, it's only going to make the situation more difficult if you call yourself a jerk (make a judgment) for having spoken to her like that. Instead, you can note that you said something to your mom that wasn't kind, that you regret it, and that you're feeling angry with yourself because of it (this is a nonjudgment). You can see that it's important here to evaluate your behavior, but evaluating in this way won't trigger extra pain for you the way judging yourself as a jerk would.

So sometimes judgments are necessary, and the point here is not to completely eliminate them but to get you to reduce the judgments you're making that trigger more emotions.

How to Be Nonjudgmental

The first step to being nonjudgmental is to become more aware of when you're judging; remember, judgments can happen so automatically that it can sometimes be hard to notice that you are judging. One good clue that you're judging is when you notice your emotional pain start to increase out of the blue. In other words, if you're not in an emotional situation (like having an argument with someone), but you suddenly start to feel guilty or ashamed, angry, hurt, bitter, or frustrated, or another painful emotion, this is a good indicator that you might be judging. Once you notice the judgment, you also have the option of just letting it go—recognizing that it's not helpful and choosing *not* to judge. Of course, the more emotions a situation triggers for us, the less likely we'll be able to go this route, but you might notice that you're more able to do this with practice.

If you can't let it go, the second step is to change your judgment when you notice it, making it a neutral statement instead. This can be the really tricky part, because you still want to express your feelings and your opinions about what's going on, but you want to do it without making things worse by judging. So how do you do this? You stick to the facts of the situation and you talk about how you feel about it.

One reason judgments aren't helpful is that they provide us with so little information. For example, imagine you get angry with your friend because he's not listening to what you're trying to tell him. He keeps talking over you, and finally you get fed up and tell him he's being a jerk. But you're not being clear about why you think he's a jerk, and you're not telling your friend what he could do differently to not be a jerk. You're not giving him helpful feedback; you're actually just making things worse, since now he'll likely get angry with you and things will escalate. To avoid going down this path, you could tell him that you're feeling frustrated because it doesn't seem like he's listening to what you're saying. This is a nonjudgmental statement—you're sticking to the facts of the situation while still expressing your feelings about what's going on. Even better, you're giving your friend information he can use to change what he's doing (if he chooses to) so that you won't feel frustrated with him anymore.

Let's look at another example. Imagine that you're having an argument with your sister. You want to borrow her sweater, and she's refusing to let you. You might tell your sister she's being "unfair," which would be a judgment. A nonjudgmental way of saying the same thing would be something like "I'm irritated and disappointed because you won't let me borrow your sweater." Putting it this way might not get you what you want, but it is unlikely to make the situation worse, because you're expressing yourself assertively. In contrast, telling your sister how unfair she is will likely only anger her and will make it even less likely that you'll get your way.

Again, judgments are a shorthand for saying something; we tend to just stick a judgmental label on something rather than saying what we really mean. Being nonjudgmental is the opposite; it is a clear, assertive way of communicating.

20 Turning a Judgment into a Nonjudgment

The following statements are all judgments. Read them and see if you can come up with a nonjudgmental statement for each. When you're done, you might want to have someone you trust check what you've written to make sure you stuck to the facts and your feelings in each situation. The first one has been done for you as an example.

You're driving down the road and someone cuts you off.

Judgment: You stupid idiot!

Nonjudgment: I can't believe that guy just cut me off! He scared me to death, and I'm so angry that he almost ran me off the road!

You get your report card back, and you got a B in math.

Judgment: I should have gotten higher marks on my report card.

Nonjudgment: _____

You missed your curfew last night, and your parents are grounding you for two weeks.

Judgment: My parents can be so mean sometimes.

Nonjudgment: _____

One of the popular kids in school is having a party, and you weren't invited.
Judgment: I'm a loser.
Nonjudgment: _____

Here are a couple more examples of judgments. See if you can come up with a nonjudgmental statement for each one:
Judgment: R & B music (or another type of music you like) is the best.
Nonjudgment: _____

Judgment: (An author you really like) is an awesome writer.
Nonjudgment: _____

Being Nonjudgmental with Yourself

As you are learning and thinking about judgments, you may find yourself thinking that you really don't judge others as much as you judge yourself. What's the problem with being self-judgmental? When your judgments are turned inward, you are still increasing the amount of pain you have. Many of us have experienced bullies in our lives, to one extent or another. When you're judging yourself, you're being a bully—toward yourself! Rest assured, this is not unusual; you've probably heard the saying, "We can be our own worst enemy." What that means is that we're often tougher on ourselves than we are on other people; many people have a hard time being kind and compassionate to themselves. When you're judging yourself, though, the results are possibly even more damaging than when you're judging others.

Let's look at an example. You get a grade that you're not happy with, and this time, instead of judging the teacher, you judge yourself: *I can't do anything right. I'm never going to be good enough to get into a good college. I'm stupid.* How do you think these kinds of thoughts are going to make you feel? Probably angry with yourself, sad or disappointed, maybe anxious, and perhaps guilty or ashamed. Now ask yourself this: what if you had a friend or a roommate who said these things to you? Would you take it? Would you fight back? Hopefully you would stand up for yourself—and that's what being nonjudgmental with yourself is about. It's about putting an end to the self-bullying.

Self-judgments are typically harder to catch because they happen more automatically for us—it's like we have a little tape recorder that runs in the back of our head, that plays those self-judgments over and over. We also don't say them out loud as often as we might other judgments, so we don't have the same awareness of judging ourselves. Therefore, the first thing I would suggest, if you know this is a problem for you, is to work on this skill more broadly: practice noticing judgments generally; work on using nonjudgmental language, changing those judgments to neutral statements. Once you have a degree of comfort using this skill in your life, you can start to really focus on changing your self-judgments. For most people, the option I mentioned earlier of just letting the judgment go is much more difficult when it comes to self-judgments, so here is an exercise to help you work on changing your self-judgments to nonjudgmental statements.

21 Changing Your Self-Judgments

First, identify one judgment you often say to yourself, and write it here: _____

_____

Now, write some details about why you're judging yourself this way; what are the facts of the situation?

_____
_____

Next, see if you can identify the feelings that cause you to judge yourself in this way, and write them here:

_____

_____

Finally, using the same formula you used before, putting these facts and feelings together, see if you can write some nonjudgmental statements to yourself:

Nonjudgment 1: _____
Nonjudgment 2: _____
Nonjudgment 3: _____

This might be difficult, so ask someone you trust for help if you need to. You can also think of that person who represents the wise self to you, and consider what they might say to you if they knew you were judging yourself this way. Or you can think of someone in your life you really care about (your best friend, sibling, even a pet), and write down what you would say to them if they were saying these things to themselves. If you're really struggling with this, don't judge yourself! That's just a really good sign that this is something you need to put a lot of work into; it will start to come naturally over time. Of course, practice will help you change the negative self-talk you've developed, so once you've written out your nonjudgmental statements, you'll need to read them to yourself regularly to increase your self-compassion.

Hopefully by now you're seeing that, although judgments can be hard to catch, working on this skill can really help you reduce the painful emotions in your life, which will increase your ability to manage your emotions.

Self-Validation

Being nonjudgmental in general will help you manage your emotions more effectively. Since you won't be generating extra pain for yourself by adding fuel to the fire of your painful emotions, your bucket of emotions won't be as full on a regular basis. The skill of self-validation will also be very helpful in this way. In this context, *self-validation* refers to being nonjudgmental with your emotions.

Have you ever noticed yourself judging your emotions? For example, maybe you feel angry at someone, but you think you *"shouldn't"* feel that way, or you tell yourself to "suck it up" and get over it. Or you might notice that you think of your painful emotions as "bad," and you try to find ways to get rid of them. This is called *invalidating* yourself, and it usually just makes you feel worse, not better. Let's look at an example.

Caleb's Story

Caleb's girlfriend broke up with him after they had been dating for about two months. He had really cared about her and was very hurt and sad that she didn't feel the same way. At the same time, though, he thought it was "stupid" that he was so down about it. He kept telling himself that she wasn't worth it and he had to just get over it, that feeling down like this was just dumb. Then he would start to feel angry with himself for feeling so down, which of course just made him feel worse—now he was feeling hurt and sad about the breakup, and he was feeling angry with himself on top of that.

Can you see that Caleb was angry at himself because he was judging himself for his feelings? This is what happens when we invalidate ourselves. How do you do in this department—do you tend to validate or invalidate yourself? The next exercise will help you think about this a bit more.

22 Do You Validate or Invalidate Yourself?

We all have times when we're able to validate ourselves and times when we find this harder. This can depend on the situation, the people involved, and, perhaps most importantly, the emotion we're feeling. Look at the following list of emotions. Think about each one carefully, then put a check mark beside the ones you tend to validate—in other words, you don't judge yourself for having them and you think it's okay when you feel this way (not that you necessarily like the feeling, but that you can see you have a right to feel this way). Use the blank lines to write in any other emotions you'd like to add to the list.

- Angry
- Anxious
- Relaxed
- Annoyed
- Down
- Irritated
- Depressed
- Frustrated
- Panicky
- Resentful
- Happy
- Excited
- Ecstatic
- Nervous
- Afraid
- Hurt
- Furious
- Stressed
- Worried
- Unhappy
- Overjoyed
- Grieving
- Bitter
- Sad
- Lonely
- Calm

Heartbroken
Scared

_____

_____

_____

Next, go back over the list again, this time putting an *X* beside those emotions you think you *in*validate—the ones you judge yourself for having. As in many of these exercises, you may find you need to experience some of these feelings before you know what you think and feel about having them. Most of us aren't used to really thinking about how we think and feel. If this is the case for you, come back to this exercise after you've experienced these emotions and can identify whether you tend to validate or invalidate yourself for having them.

Messages We Receive About Emotions

Once you're able to identify *how* you think and feel about your emotions, it can help to think about *why* you think and feel this way. We often receive messages from our family, our friends, and even society in general about our feelings. For example, your parents might tell you, "It's not nice to be angry;" your friends might say, "Enough already; just get over it" when you're feeling sad; and society provides us with stereotypical messages such as "Boys don't cry." Take a look at the following stories about some people who received certain messages in their lives about emotions. These stories are meant to get you thinking about where your own thoughts and beliefs about emotions are coming from.

Tyler's and Brandon's Stories

Tyler's parents separated when he was ten. He remembered them arguing a lot even before then. His father would often come home late from work, and his mother would be angry with him for not calling to let her know. Tyler's father would keep telling his mother she had no right to be mad at him, because he was working overtime to pay their bills. He would say that she was just trying to get under his skin and that she really knew what buttons to push to make him angry.

When he was thirteen, Tyler started to have problems with anger. He would "stuff" it for as long as he could; he didn't want to express his anger, because he thought it was "bad." Eventually, though, Tyler would end up exploding and all that built-up anger would come out at once. His friends stopped spending as much time around him, because he was unpredictable; he would get angry and blow up at them for small things. It also affected his relationships with his family, and Tyler was feeling more and more alone.

Brandon grew up in a family where emotions in general weren't expressed much. If he got excited about something, he was told to settle down because he was being annoying. If he was sad, he was told to stop being weak, and if he cried, he was told he was acting like a girl, because boys didn't cry. Anger was labeled "mean" or "not nice," and anxiety was for "cowards" or "scaredy-cats." With all of these direct messages about how negative many of his emotions were, it's no wonder that Brandon had a hard time letting himself feel emotions, never mind express them! He would do everything he could to ignore, avoid, and push away his emotions, and he certainly wasn't accepting of them. He had heard these messages for so long that Brandon would judge himself when he felt these emotions.

These are just two examples of how we can develop beliefs about emotions. Sometimes the messages we receive are subtle, like in Tyler's example, where the messages weren't directly said to him but he absorbed them anyway. Other times, the messages are more direct, like Brandon's experience where he was outright told that emotions are bad. As you consider your own experiences, remember that your parents learned about emotions from their family, so we're not blaming them; we just want you to be aware of where your own beliefs come from.

23 What Messages Have You Received About Emotions?

Review the list from activity 22 and identify one of the emotions that you invalidate; write this emotion on the first blank line. Next, write down any messages you've received about this emotion, whether from your family, friends, or society. Finally, write down any thoughts and emotions you can identify that arise because of these messages. Do this for each of the emotions you invalidate, using another sheet of paper if you run out of room. The first one has been done for you as an example.

Emotion: *Anxiety*

Messages I've received about this emotion: *I shouldn't feel this way; it's silly.*

How these messages make me think and feel about having this emotion: *I think it makes me weak, and I feel ashamed about feeling anxious.*

Emotion: _____

Messages I've received about this emotion: _____

_____

_____

How these messages make me think and feel about having this emotion:

Emotion: _____
Messages I've received about this emotion:
_____
_____

How these messages make me think and feel about having this emotion: _____
_____

Emotion: _____
Messages I've received about this emotion:
_____
_____

How these messages make me think and feel about having this emotion: _____
_____

Once you've been paying attention to what you think and how you feel about your emotions for a while, you might notice that you are more able to validate yourself in spite of these old messages.

It's important to know, when we're judging ourselves for how we feel, quite often guilt and shame as well as other distressing feelings show up; so you'll likely find that validating your emotions helps reduce these distressing feelings over time. Below are three ways of validating yourself (Van Dijk 2012):

1. *Acknowledging:* This is when we just label the emotion we're feeling, accurately labeling the feeling and leaving it at that: *I feel anxious.* As long as we just name it, and we don't go further and judge it, we're validating our feeling.
2. *Allowing:* This is when we give ourselves permission to feel the feeling. We're not saying we like the emotion or that we want it to stick around; we're saying we're allowed to feel this way since this is a normal human emotion.
3. *Understanding:* This is when we can say in some way that *this feeling makes sense* given either the current circumstances or our past. For example, we could say that it's understandable to feel anxious being in situations with new people when you have a history of being bullied by others—this would be understanding the emotion based on past experiences. Or someone could say it makes sense that they feel anxious about

public speaking, because it's not something they do regularly and it's outside of their comfort zone—this would be understanding the emotion based on current experience.

24 Validating Yourself

Here are some examples of acknowledging, allowing, understanding, and validating statements. Highlight or underline the statements that would be most helpful for the emotions you tend to invalidate.
- It's okay that I feel this way.
- This is a natural human emotion.
- Everyone feels this way sometimes.
- It makes sense that I feel this way.
- I'm allowed to feel this.

In the space provided, see if you can come up with more statements that will help you think in a nonjudgmental, more balanced way about emotions that you tend to invalidate. Remember that this is not about liking the emotion or wanting to change it; rather, it's a nonjudgmental way of thinking about the emotion you're experiencing so that you don't add fuel to the fire of your emotion and trigger more pain for yourself.

_____

_____

_____

_____

Because changing your thoughts this way can be pretty hard, you might want to rewrite this list of validating statements on a separate piece of paper that you can carry with you; or add it to the notes section in your phone or tablet. That way, when you start to experience an emotion that you don't like and that you tend to invalidate, you can pull out your list and read it to yourself.

Reality Acceptance

So far in this chapter, we've looked at two skills that can help you reduce the amount of pain in your life: not judging yourself and others and not judging your emotions. The next skill similarly helps you reduce the amount of emotional pain in your life, this time by focusing on how you think about the *situation*.

When was the last time you were in a painful situation and heard yourself say, "This is so unfair. It's not right. It shouldn't be this way," or something along those lines? Did thinking about the situation this way help you? Or did it make you feel more emotions or feel your emotions more intensely? It's pretty natural for us to try to fight whatever causes us pain. When we fight reality in this way, though, it actually makes our pain worse. Take a look at the following exercise to help you think about this idea.

25 What Does Fighting Reality Do for You?

Think of a recent time when you thought something like *It's not fair* or *This shouldn't have happened* or *This sucks*. Then answer these questions: Write a brief description of the situation:

_____
_____

How did you feel when you were fighting this situation? If you have a hard time answering this question, think about these four general categories of emotions: mad, sad, scared, and happy. Also remember that you may have been feeling more than one emotion at a time. Write down whatever emotions you can identify:

_____

What did you *do* because you were fighting the situation? For example, you might have been sleeping or drinking or using drugs to escape reality more often, or maybe you cried a lot or lashed out at others because you were feeling so emotional. Whatever behaviors you can recall, write them here:

_____

_____

Can you think of any benefits that came from fighting this reality?

_____

Generally, refusing to accept a situation makes our emotions snowball, just like when we judge ourselves or others and when we invalidate our emotions. Take a look at the following example to help you understand this idea.

> **Kerri's Story**
>
> Kerri was fourteen when she started dating her first boyfriend, Brad. She totally fell for him, and they were together for about a year. Kerri thought things were going well, and she was happy in their relationship, even though they didn't get to spend much time together. But one day, out of the blue, Brad told Kerri he was seeing someone else and didn't want to be with her anymore. She tried to get him to change his mind, but to no avail.

> Kerri was devastated; she skipped school the next day because she felt so awful, and she stayed in her room all day, crying. She kept thinking that this wasn't the way it was supposed to be and that it wasn't fair that she should lose someone who made her so happy. This went on for days, and Kerri became so distraught that she cut herself, trying to distract herself with physical pain to make the emotional pain go away. It was also her way of punishing herself, because she thought she must have done something wrong for Brad to have left her and for her to feel so much emotional pain.

Most people in this situation would have felt a lot of pain. The end of a relationship is often hard, and people usually feel very sad about this kind of loss. However, you might be able to see that Kerri was fighting the situation by thinking things like *It's not fair* and *It shouldn't be this way*. This kind of thinking triggered more emotions for Kerri so that she not only felt sad about the loss but felt even worse and also became angry with herself, adding to her emotional pain and leading to unhealthy behaviors like cutting herself. Let's look at what happened next.

> As time went on, Kerri gradually began to accept that Brad had chosen to be with someone else. She came to realize that she

had no control over the situation and that, while she didn't like it, she would have to deal with it. "It is what it is" became Kerri's new mantra to help her get through the day. She found that this new attitude helped her move forward with her life. The sadness was still there and she continued to miss Brad, but she stopped blaming herself and being angry with herself, which reduced her painful emotions and made her feelings more bearable.

Fighting Reality vs. Reality Acceptance

It's often difficult to accept that painful things have happened or are happening in our lives. So instead of accepting these things, we have a tendency to fight reality, usually by trying to deny it in some way, as though by denying it or fighting it, we can make it not true. But when we refuse to accept these things, it obviously doesn't change the fact that the events have happened. Fighting reality doesn't make things better; it just ends up causing us even more pain.

Reality acceptance is when you're able to acknowledge reality as it is and act accordingly instead of fighting it and trying to turn it into something it's not. Keep in mind that *acceptance* has nothing to do with *approval*—acceptance is actually nonjudgmental. In other words, when you accept something, you're not saying it's good or bad; you're just acknowledging it. Notice that, in the story about Kerri, she was able to come to accept her situation, even though she still didn't like the way things were. So, remembering what you learned earlier in this chapter, that judgments increase your emotional pain, you can think of reality acceptance as being nonjudgmental toward reality.

What Reality Acceptance Isn't

Accepting reality does not mean that you give up, that you stop trying to change a situation, or that you become passive. For example, if your parents make a decision that's painful for you, acceptance doesn't mean that you simply sit back without trying to do anything about it; you can both accept that this is their decision *and* talk to them about the situation to see if you can get them to change their minds.

Quite often we have no control over a situation, which can make it more painful. When someone we love dies, we have no control. Past situations are another example. Many people feel regret, guilt, shame, and anger at themselves about things they did, things they didn't do, or things that were done to them in the past. But we have no control over these events, no ability to go into the past and change things. When you can't do anything about the outcome, acceptance helps you move on. While acceptance won't change reality and therefore won't take all of your pain away, it will help reduce the amount of pain you're experiencing.

26 How Reality Acceptance Helps

Based on the situation you used in activity 25, answer the following questions to help you think about how accepting reality can help you.

Have you gotten to the point where you can accept that situation, even if only for short periods of time? If so, how has this helped you?

_____
_____

If you haven't been able to accept this situation yet, try to think of another painful time in your life (for example, the death of a family member, friend, or pet; or the loss of a relationship or friendship) where you were able to gradually get to acceptance. Can you recall how accepting this situation helped you? Here are some examples; add your own on the blank lines that follow:
- I started to think about the situation less often.
- My anger toward myself lessened.
- I stopped avoiding certain people.
  - _____
  - _____
  - _____

Do you have other past or present situations in your life that you're not accepting? Write down any situations you can identify that you're fighting; use another piece of paper if you need more room.

_____
_____
_____

Thinking about each of these situations, one at a time, how do you think it could be helpful for you to accept the situation? For example, would it change how you feel or reduce the level of your emotion? Will it change the way you're behaving?

_____
_____
_____
_____
_____

Next, pick one of the situations that you're still having trouble accepting. Sometimes you might find you need to accept your nonacceptance! In other words, if you're struggling to get to a place where you're willing to work on accepting something, you can practice accepting that you're not yet ready to accept it. If you beat yourself up and judge yourself for not doing something that you know would be helpful, yet again you're just adding fuel to that emotional fire. So accept that you're not yet ready to accept this situation: it is what it is.

However, if you're finding yourself ready to work on acceptance with that situation, make a commitment to yourself here:

As of this moment, I'm going to start working on accepting the following situation:

_____

_____

You're also going to notice at times that your mind has returned to fighting that reality. Consider how you can talk back to those thoughts, the things you could you say to yourself to help you accept this situation. Again, here are some examples and some blank lines where you can add your own ideas:

- It is what it is.
- It's hard right now, but I can get through it.
- I don't like it, but there's nothing I can do to change it.
- _____
- _____
- _____

Again, mindfulness will be helpful here. You need to first increase your awareness of when you are fighting this reality; then, when you find your thoughts turning in that direction, you can say some of your reality-acceptance statements to yourself. It's important to remember that this is not an easy skill—the more painful a situation is, the harder it will be for you to accept.

For really painful situations, you might also find that breaking them down into smaller parts can help with acceptance: for example, instead of trying to accept that your parents are divorcing, maybe you can work on first accepting just one part of this: that one of your parents is no longer living at home with you. The next step might be to work on accepting that you can no longer have family holidays, birthdays, and so on with both of your parents at the same time; then might come accepting that you now have to split your time between two houses; and so forth. Remember that even though it's difficult and typically takes a lot of energy, in the long run, accepting reality will pay off!

On the other hand, if you're trying to accept something that's really painful, it also may be just too much right now: you might need to consider taking a step back and practicing this skill first with something that's much less painful. Although, of course, we usually want to do something about the intense pain in our lives, sometimes a situation might have too much pain attached to it for us to be able to get to the point of using skills effectively right away. If this turns out to be the case, think about less painful, even daily events that you can practice accepting: when your brother leaves his dishes in the sink or when your parents get on your case about cutting the grass "now please" ... or the fact that it's Saturday morning and it's raining. There are usually lots of things to find that cause relatively small amounts of pain and provide good practice!

Practicing mindfulness will help you with all three skills of being nonjudgmental, self-validation, and reality acceptance. Because our thoughts are often so automatic, they can be very difficult for us to catch—we often have very little or even no awareness of what we're thinking. So return to activity 12 in chapter 2 to increase your awareness of your judgments, of what you say to yourself about your emotions, and of when you're fighting reality.

27 Loving-Kindness Meditation

The skills we've talked about in this chapter are very difficult, but practicing them will help you feel less emotional pain and be kinder to yourself. This mindfulness exercise (Brantley and Hanauer 2008) can also help you be kinder to yourself. It focuses on self-compassion, but as you get used to this kind of mindfulness practice, you may also want to extend these kind thoughts to others.

Find a place to sit where you'll be comfortable. Begin by focusing on your breathing—not trying to change your breath but just noticing how it feels to breathe. Slowly, deeply, and comfortably, inhale and exhale.

As you focus on your breathing, allow yourself to connect with pleasurable feelings—feelings of kindness, friendliness, warmth, and compassion. These are the feelings you experience when you see a person you really care about; when your pet comes to greet you; when you do something nice for someone "just because." Recall that warmth and kindness you experience toward others; imagine those feelings right now, as though they were happening in this moment, and let yourself feel the joy, love, and other pleasurable feelings that come up for you. As you experience these feelings of kindness and friendliness, gently say the following words:

May I be happy.

May I be healthy.

May I be peaceful.

May I be safe.

You can say these words in your head or out loud; either way, put feeling and meaning into them, and make sure that you really feel the words as you say them. If you have a hard time feeling kindness toward yourself, remember that habits take time to change—as best as you can, do not judge yourself or the exercise but just know that this is something you'll need to spend more time on. Make sure that you practice this exercise regularly, and you will find yourself taking a more kind, loving, and compassionate attitude toward yourself, which will help you be nonjudgmental toward yourself, to validate the emotions you're feeling, and to accept your reality.

Wrapping Up

In this chapter, we've covered a lot of skills to help you reduce the amount of pain in your life. By trying to be less judgmental, by working on validating your emotions more often, and by working toward accepting painful situations in your life, you will be able to reduce the amount of emotional pain you experience. Remember that when you have less emotional pain, your emotions become more manageable. Gradually, you'll begin to notice that you're lashing out at others less often and that you're more able to manage your emotions in effective ways, instead of resorting to the unhealthy ways that you've used to try to cope with them in the past. Take your time and work hard on these skills, and you will notice a difference.

CHAPTER FIVE

Surviving a Crisis Without Making It Worse

We all have times in our lives when our emotions get intense and we don't know how to deal with them. Quite often when this happens, we experience urges to do things that might help us cope with our overwhelming feelings in the short term but have some negative consequences in the long run. The skills in this chapter will help you cope in healthier ways so that you'll be able to get through a crisis situation without making it worse.

Tameka's Story

Tameka was thirteen when she began to have problems with her emotions. At times she would get so depressed that she just wanted to die. Other times, especially after she had lashed out at her family or friends because she felt so sad and angry, she would hurt herself in some way—she would cut herself or pinch herself really hard. It was almost as if inflicting pain on herself was punishment for the way she was taking things out on the people she loved. But at the same time, the physical pain served as a distraction from her emotional pain. Even though Tameka knew her way of coping was unhealthy, she just couldn't let go of it—she knew it usually helped, at least at first, and falling back on these old patterns was easier than trying to change. Gradually, though, Tameka's family and friends became more and more frustrated with her because it seemed like she didn't want to help herself. Tameka did want to help herself; she just didn't know how.

Does this sound at all familiar? Maybe you don't have thoughts of killing or hurting yourself, but we've all tried to get through intense emotions by doing things that have ended up just making things worse. Some people drink or use drugs; some people overeat or undereat; others sleep, play video games all day, or do other things to help them escape their reality. The skills in this chapter will help you stop resorting to these unhelpful behaviors and replace them with coping skills that have no negative consequences, either short or long term. First, let's take a look at what you currently do to help you cope with crisis situations.

28 How Do You Cope?

The difficult thing about changing unhealthy ways of coping is that they are often helpful in the short term. When your emotions are really intense and you don't know how to get through a crisis, many of these behaviors distract you from the situation and from your emotions. But remember, this doesn't last. In the long run, the crisis is still there, and your emotions about it are still there, but now you're likely to have more pain because of the unhealthy behavior you engaged in—usually, people feel guilt, shame, and anger toward themselves when they've engaged in these kinds of behaviors. In addition, your loved ones will likely get frustrated with you, as Tameka's did with her, because you're acting in ways that are more harmful to you.

Look at this list of unhealthy ways of coping and check off the ones you sometimes resort to. Use the blank lines at the end to add other behaviors you turn to that you know aren't helpful in the long run.

- ☐ Cutting yourself
- ☐ Threatening suicide
- ☐ Using sleep to escape
- ☐ Drinking alcohol
- ☐ Using drugs
- ☐ Gambling
- ☐ Playing video games excessively
- ☐ Thinking about suicide
- ☐ Lashing out at people you care about
- ☐ Not eating
- ☐ Eating too much
- ☐ Attempting suicide

☐ Pulling out your hair
☐ Pinching yourself
☐ Becoming violent toward others
☐ Throwing things
☐ Banging your head against a wall
☐ Engaging in dangerous sexual practices (for example, having unprotected sex or having sex with someone you just met)
☐ _____
☐ _____
☐ _____

Choose one of these behaviors that you do relatively frequently. Can you identify triggers or factors that put you at risk for this behavior? Describe any events, people, or other circumstances that increase the chance that you'll engage in this behavior:

_____
_____
_____

Write about how this behavior is helpful for you when you're in a crisis.

_____
_____
_____

Can you think of any negative consequences this behavior has for you? This can be hard because, as noted above, this behavior probably helps you in the short term, so you might need to ask someone you trust for assistance. Write any negative consequences you can think of here:

_____
_____
_____

We tend to be much harder on ourselves than we would be on others, so sometimes it can help if we talk to ourselves like we would talk to a friend in the same situation. Imagine that you are your best friend, a close family member, or even your pet. From this other perspective, write a letter to yourself about the unhealthy ways you currently cope. Tell how this behavior affects you (as your loved one), and offer encouragement for doing things differently. Use another piece of paper if you need more room.

_____
_____
_____
_____
_____
_____
_____

It's likely that you've also had times when you've been in a crisis and have acted in ways that don't affect you negatively. Sometimes it just feels helpful to get out and take a walk, talk to someone, or watch a movie, for example, to get your mind off the crisis and your painful emotions. In the following space, list some of these things you've done to help you cope in healthy ways:

_____

_____

_____

Now let's look at how you can start moving away from those unhealthy behaviors and make it more likely you'll be able to cope in more helpful ways. The following section is adapted from Van Dijk (2021).

Change Your Emotion by Changing Your Body

A good place to start when you notice your emotions taking over is to focus on changing what's happening in your body. Here are some techniques that will help you quickly reregulate emotions, getting you to a more emotionally balanced place where you'll be able to think from your wise self.

Doing a Forward Bend

Bend over as though you're trying to touch your toes (it doesn't matter if you can actually touch your toes; and you can also do this sitting down if you'd like). Focus on taking slow, deep breaths and just let yourself hang out there for a little while. This activates a system in the body known as the *parasympathetic nervous system*, which serves as the body's brake, helping us to feel a little calmer. Just don't stand up too quickly, or you might fall over.

Sticking Your Face in Cold Water

If you're not taking medications called beta blockers, and you don't have problems with low blood pressure or disordered eating (restricting or purging), putting your face in cold water is another skill that can help reregulate your emotions fast (Linehan 2014). (If you're not sure if this is okay for you, be sure to check with your doctor; this skill can actually cause you to pass out, so please be careful!)

Go to the nearest sink, fill it with water as cold as it will go, and put your face in the water for about fifteen to thirty seconds (if you can't hold your breath that long, don't worry, but go as long as you comfortably can). If you can't put cold water in a sink (or if there's a fear about this for you), you can also splash cold water on your face or hold an ice pack over your eyes, but this will still work best if you hold your breath and tip yourself over as though you were putting your face in water. You might want to do this two or three times to help settle your emotions fast.

Focusing on Your Exhale

Focusing on making your exhale longer than your inhale also activates the parasympathetic nervous system, helping you to slow down and feel calmer. Here's how to do this: As you slowly inhale, count in your head to see how long your inhale is.

Then, as you exhale, count at the same pace and make sure your exhale is at least a little bit longer than your inhale. For example, if you get to five when you inhale, make sure you exhale to at least six; if you count only to three when you inhale, you'll want your exhale to be at least to the count of four. Try doing this for a few minutes at a time to help calm intense emotions.

Increasing Your Heart Rate Through Exercise

Doing some intense exercise can also help you reregulate emotions when they start to intensify—or even if they're already intense! Go for a run or walk as fast as you can; do some jumping jacks or push-ups in your bedroom; or run up and down your stairs. Intense exercise gives the chemicals in the brain a boost and helps manage emotions.

Keep in mind that these skills will only reregulate your emotions for a short time (about five to fifteen minutes). I think of doing these things as a way of temporarily getting unhijacked from your emotions so that you'll be able to access your wise self and therefore be able to think a little more clearly about how to help yourself not make the situation worse (for example, by acting on urges to hurt yourself or someone else). This is where the next sets of skills come in.

Distracting Skills

When you're in a crisis situation, you might not be able to solve the problem you're facing. If you can, obviously you want to solve it, and the crisis will disappear! But when it's a problem that can't be solved, and your emotions about it are therefore going to keep hanging around, one of the most helpful things you can do is distract yourself from the problem, and to do this in a way that is not going to make things worse for you in the long run. Your list of healthy ways of coping (see the end of activity 28) is likely a list of distracting skills, because on some level, even when it's hard for us to think straight because we're so emotional, we know that distracting ourselves will help us feel better, even if it's only temporary.

29 Distracting Yourself

Read this list of activities to get you thinking about what you can do to get your mind off a problem and your emotions. On a separate sheet of paper, make your own list to keep with you, and use it to distract yourself when you're in a crisis.

Draw, paint, or doodle.
Look at photographs.
Write a poem or short story.
Think of times when you felt happy.
Sing or dance.
Look at old yearbooks.
Imagine your life after school.
Go to a movie.
Spend time outdoors.
List the things you like about yourself.
Upload some favorite photos on Snapchat.
Play a board game with your sibling or a friend.
Find a fun new ring tone for your cell.
Cook or bake something for your family.
Watch a movie or your favorite show.
Go somewhere to people watch.
Reach out to someone you miss.
Update your Instagram status.
Listen to music or a relaxation exercise.
Spend time with a friend.

Experiment with different hairstyles.

Close your eyes and imagine yourself in your favorite place.

Play a musical instrument.

Learn how to crochet (or something else new).

Journal.

Play a sport you enjoy.

Do something nice for your family or a friend.

Rearrange or organize your bedroom.

Do a crossword puzzle.

Not all of these activities will make sense for you; for example, if you don't play a sport, it would make no sense to have this activity on your list. So think really hard and make your own list of as many activities as you can think of. That way, when you start to notice warning signs of an impending crisis, or when you're actually in a crisis, you won't have to think about what you can do to help yourself—you can just pick up this list of crisis survival skills and do the first thing on it. If you find that this activity only distracts you for a few minutes, or perhaps not at all, then move on to the next activity. The more options you have, the more you'll be able to distract yourself, and the more likely you'll be able to get through the crisis without making it worse. Don't forget to add the skills to change your emotion by changing your body—these should go to the top of your list!

Soothing Skills

Taking good care of yourself physically is an important way to reduce emotional crises. Being able to take care of your mental health by soothing yourself—doing things to help you relax, feel calmer, and be at peace—is equally important. Self-soothing can help during times of crisis, and it should also be something you do on a regular basis to prevent crises from occurring. Think about it: if you're regularly doing things that help you feel calmer and more relaxed, you'll be better able to handle stressful situations when they do arise, so they won't have the same opportunity to escalate into crises.

In coming up with ways to soothe yourself, think of things you can do that are comforting for you. For example, if you have a dog, being with it could be soothing for you. Perhaps you like to sit with your dog, pet it, and enjoy its company. These activities will be different for everyone.

30 Soothing Yourself

Think about things you may have done in the past to help yourself feel better, like asking someone for a hug, taking a hot bath, or snuggling under the blankets with a good book. You can also think about what is pleasing to each of your senses—taste, touch, sight, smell, and hearing—and what you can do that is soothing to each sense (Linehan 1993). For example, it's soothing for some people to eat their favorite food (in reasonable amounts, of course!), to pet their dog, to look at a garden, to smell fresh-baked bread, and to hear the voice of someone dear to them.

What is soothing for you? Add what you come up with to your list of crisis survival skills. Here are some more examples to help you get started:

Drinking a cup of hot chocolate

Listening to your favorite music

Enjoying the scent of flowers

Listening to nature sounds

Looking at a favorite object

Soaking in a hot bubble bath

Using aromatherapy

Making a Safety Box

In times of crisis, having some of your favorite things handy can help you soothe yourself and feel calmer. You can get creative and put together a container of some sort that holds many of your favorite things. Below is a

list of things that some people have included in their safety boxes:
- Photos of family and friends
- A favorite stuffed animal
- Body lotion
- A baseball card
- A pet rock
- Dried flowers
- A favorite book
- An inspiring poem
- A souvenir from a trip with happy memories

Steps to Managing Your Urge

Now it's time to put all of these skills together with the following steps to help you not act on an urge that would likely make the situation worse for you.

Step one. Notice your urge and rate it on a scale of 1 to 10 (1 means it's there, but barely noticeable; 10 means it's super intense and you're likely to act on it).

Step two. Set an alarm for fifteen minutes—on your phone or tablet, or use the oven timer in the kitchen if you need to! Promise yourself that for the next fifteen minutes you're going to use skills instead of acting on the urge.

Step three. Pull out your list of crisis survival skills and do the first thing on the list (remember, this should be one of those body-chemistry changing skills, like a forward bend, to help you get reregulated). Once you've hopefully gotten your emotions to quiet down at least a little bit—and even if for some reason you couldn't to do that—your next step is to use the rest of your skills: distract yourself from the urge and use your self-soothing skills to get you through the crisis. If the first distracting skill on your list is "go for a walk," but it's midnight and not safe for you to walk alone, move on to the next thing. If the next thing is "watch Netflix," but you can't even focus on your favorite show right now, go on to the next thing. This is why you want your list to be as long as possible. Some skills are going to be more effective at certain times than others, but the key is to keep using the skills until your timer goes off. Remember, you want to delay acting on the urge, to get you through the crisis without making it worse.

Step four. When the timer goes off after fifteen minutes, rate your urge again. If it's lower, hopefully you can pat yourself on the back for a job well done and continue with your day. If the urge has stayed the same or even increased, ideally you will set the timer for another fifteen minutes and return to using more skills. This can be really difficult, and the truth is it won't always happen; but even if you do end up acting on your urge, you still need to give yourself credit for using skills first instead of acting on automatic pilot like you normally would have. This is progress, and over time you'll be more able to use these skills to resist acting on the urge. It's hard work, it takes lots of practice, and, as you hopefully already know, it will be worth it in the long run.

Crisis Plans

In a crisis situation, it can be tough to think straight—your emotions take over, and you want to do what's comfortable and easy, even if it's not what's going to be helpful in the long run. You can help yourself by having an idea of your risk factors (the people, places, or things that trigger emotional stress for you) and of the warning signs that you are getting into a crisis or losing control. For example, your risk factors might include fighting with your parents or hanging around with certain people whom you always end up arguing with; your warning signs might be that you stop caring about school and no longer do homework or that you isolate yourself and sleep more. You'll also want to think about what you can do to help yourself and who else can be contacted to help you.

With a crisis plan in place, you don't have to think about what to do when you're in crisis—you just refer to your plan, and it tells you what to do!

31 Creating a Crisis Plan

As you fill out your plan, you may want to refer to your list of distracting and self-soothing skills. It can also be helpful to share this plan with your support people, those in your life with whom you're comfortable talking about your problems and know you can count on in times of crisis; this could be a parent, your best friend, a favorite aunt or uncle, or a Big Sister or Big Brother. You can also download this crisis plan at http://www.newharbinger.com/47360.

Crisis Plan

Name: _____

My risk factors or triggers are:

_____

_____

_____

When I am getting into crisis, or feel like I'm losing control, some of the warning signs are:

_____

_____

_____

To help me quickly get reregulated, I can:

To help me distract from the crisis, I can:
_____
_____

To soothe myself, I can:
_____
_____

My support people:
Person to call _____ Phone number _____
Situation to call in _____
Person to call _____ Phone number _____
Situation to call in _____
Person to call _____ Phone number _____
Situation to call in _____
Person to call _____ Phone number _____
Situation to call in _____

Crisis hotline to call, text, or email when no one else is available (for example, in the middle of the night):

Other information that might be useful for people who are helping me in a crisis (for example, information about my family and other people who are important to me; my goals, hobbies, interests; and so on):
_____

Names and telephone numbers of other people to contact (if applicable):
Psychiatrist: _____
Family doctor: _____
Guidance counselor, case manager, psychotherapist, or other involved professionals:
_____

Parents, caregivers, or other trusted people who could be contacted in case of emergency:
_____

Wrapping Up

One of the biggest reasons crisis situations can be so hard to get through without making things worse is that we usually don't plan ahead for them. This means that we end up falling back on those old, easy, comfortable, but unhealthy ways of coping. By working your way through this chapter—learning how to reregulate, making a list of crisis survival skills, creating a safety box, and filling out your crisis plan—you've planned ahead. Now you just need to make sure you keep these things handy so that when you begin experiencing a crisis, you can pull out your list of skills and just start doing them—minimal thinking involved!

As you use these skills over time, you'll find that the number of crises you experience decreases because you're more capable of handling stress and other uncomfortable emotions and also because you'll stop making things worse in a crisis, which in the past probably led to more crises. No longer falling back into those old patterns of behavior also means more support from your family and friends when they see that you really are trying hard to make changes in your life and in the way you manage your emotions.

CHAPTER SIX

Improving Your Mood

So far in this workbook you've learned skills to help you manage emotions that are painful as well as skills to help you prevent extra emotional pain from arising. But even though you're doing these things—and hopefully feeling better and feeling proud of yourself for your accomplishments—it's important to realize that, if you're regularly feeling depressed, anxious, angry, or experiencing other painful emotions, it will take some additional work for your mood to improve. So this chapter is about what you can do to help you increase your *pleasurable* emotions.

Moods Don't Improve Without Effort

Quite often when you're feeling depressed, anxious, angry, or any other kind of emotional pain, you don't feel like doing things. But here's the catch: unless you do enjoyable things, you're not going to start feeling better. As hard as it can sometimes be to do something that could be enjoyable when you're feeling down, it's an important way to help yourself stop feeling down!

When you're not doing enjoyable things, boredom can also set in, which can cause more problems. Look at Robert's story to help this idea make sense.

Robert's Story

Robert was fifteen years old when he started to have problems with anxiety. About a year later he was also diagnosed with bipolar disorder. He spent some time in the hospital, which was really hard on him, and what made things even worse was that he lost a lot of his friends. He missed out on most of senior year, and when he finally got back to school, most of his friends had graduated and moved on. Robert managed to graduate from high school, and his bipolar disorder was finally under control, but he continued to have a hard time with anxiety. He started college but decided to do only one course at a time to make it more manageable. He also got a part-time job at a retail store. But even going to school one day a week, and working two to three days each week, Robert was bored. He didn't have enough to fill his time, which led to other problems—he started to eat a lot more than usual out of boredom, and this feeling of boredom (and the weight he gained from eating more) made him feel more down.

Boredom often leads to unhealthy behaviors, like Robert's increased eating. Having too much time on your hands can also leave you with too much time to think, or dwell on things, which can also bring your mood down, and this in turn can lead to other unhealthy urges and behaviors. Hopefully you're starting to see the importance of increasing the amount of activity in your life!

32 Things You Enjoy

What are some things you can do that might give your mood the opportunity to improve? Make sure you're not aiming too high: these activities may very well help you feel a little happier, relaxed, or content, or they may actually be fun, but sometimes it will be helpful to think instead about what will be calming, peaceful, satisfying, or perhaps give you a sense of pleasure or contentment. This activity will help you think about these things and then start incorporating them into your life so that over time you'll feel better. Make a list of activities you like, whether it's something you're currently doing or something you used to do that was fun or helped you to feel relaxed or content. The following examples can start you off. Circle any of the following activities that apply and add your own ideas on the blank lines.

Playing with your dog

Playing a sport

Reading

Taking photographs

Going to the movies

Going for a walk

Painting

Playing paintball

Spending time with friends

Be sure to use another piece of paper if you run out of room—the more activities you can come up with, the better.

How many times in one week do you do any of these activities? _____

Ideally, you want to do something like this *every single day!* It doesn't have to be a gigantic thing you do, and you don't have to spend a lot of time doing it, but the more often you can incorporate these kinds of activities into your life—even if you aren't getting the same amount of enjoyment out of them as you used to—the quicker your mood will start to improve.

If you don't already have things you could do every day, think of activities you might like to do. Use the space below (and extra paper if you need more room) to brainstorm. Be creative, and don't limit yourself; if an activity pops into your mind as something that might be fun, relaxing, enjoyable, or interesting, write it down even if it seems unrealistic, like traveling or learning to fly.

_____
_____
_____
_____

Quite often we have things we'd like to do that aren't always possible for some reason—we don't have the time, can't afford it, aren't old enough, or whatever. But just because we can't do that exact thing doesn't mean there aren't ways to experience similar things. For example, if you've always wanted to take a photography class but don't have the money, you could find an interest group on websites like Pinterest or meetup.com, where others might be able to share their knowledge for free; if you can't find an interest group, start one! Read books on photography. See if you can find local photographers to speak to about what they did to get started. Think outside the box and remember that sometimes planning can be just as much fun as doing the activity itself.

Next, pick one thing from your list above, and see if you can come up with a plan to engage in that activity or something similar, using the following questions to help you:

What is the activity you'd most like to do from your list? Write it here: _____

Is there anything preventing you from doing this activity? If so, what? _____

_____

_____

If there's nothing preventing you from doing the activity, go ahead and make plans to do it. If you are unable to do the activity for some reason, what else might you be able to do to help you learn more about it or perhaps to experience it in a different way? If you're not sure, ask someone you trust for help.

_____

_____

_____

Your next step, of course, is to start to engage in some of these activities.

Building Mastery

It's important not only to do activities that might give your mood the opportunity to improve but also that make you feel productive, like you're accomplishing something. This is the DBT skill known as *building mastery* (Linehan 1993). The activities that give us a sense of mastery will be different for every single person. For one person, it could be getting up in the morning and getting to school on time. For someone else, it could be working at a part-time job, going to the gym, doing volunteer work, or making it to volleyball practice. For someone else, it could be socializing—getting together with friends, or going to a party. The activity doesn't matter so much as the feeling you get from it—that sense of accomplishment, of being able to say to yourself, *Hey, look what I did*. The feeling you're after when you build mastery is that of having challenged yourself and being proud of yourself for having done it. Oliver's story is an example.

Oliver's Story

Oliver's mom had died a year ago, and since then he had been having problems controlling his anger. He would often lash out at his father—even when he knew it wasn't really his dad he was angry with—because he was still sad and angry over the loss of his mother. Oliver began to practice mindfulness and the other skills outlined in this book to help him manage his emotions better. Gradually, he found that he was feeling more in control and he was lashing out at his dad less. Instead of letting his anger get the best of him, Oliver was often able to stop himself from reacting. He would take some time to get himself feeling calmer and then talk to his dad about what was bothering him. This change gave Oliver a feeling of mastery—he was proud of himself for being able to change his behavior and felt good about his accomplishment.

33 What Can You Do to Build Mastery?

Remember, building mastery will be different for everyone. You might find that some of the pleasurable activities you already came up with will give you a sense of accomplishment, so there may be some overlap. Use the following space to list some activities that you think will both challenge you and help you feel good about yourself. Here are some ideas to get you started; circle any that make sense for you, and then add your own ideas on the blank lines.

Volunteering at a food bank

Getting yourself to school on time

Getting an average of at least a B in math

Practicing the skills you're learning in this book

Shoveling your neighbor's driveway

Getting your chores done on time

Going out with a group of friends

_____

_____

_____

If you're have a hard time thinking about what will give you that feeling of pride or accomplishment, try thinking about the things that make you feel good about yourself. Ask yourself what you would tell a friend who was trying to think of ways to improve her self-esteem. And don't forget, you can always ask someone you trust for help.

The Importance of Setting Goals

Quite often, reaching a goal has the effect of building mastery—not only will you enjoy finally doing what you set out to do, but you'll also have a sense of accomplishment for getting there. You'll feel some kind of pleasurable emotions—maybe happiness, contentment, or pride—for reaching that goal. You'll feel better about yourself, and this, in turn, will have a positive impact on your mood. Having goals that you're striving toward and looking forward to helps improve your mood and can also help keep you from acting on urges to do things that would be harmful to you.

Aisha's Story

Aisha had been struggling with an eating disorder. She knew that her behavior was unhealthy and that she was sacrificing a lot to maintain her disordered eating—her relationships were being affected, and not eating also caused other problems, such as depression and difficulties with concentration and memory. But Aisha continued to struggle with the idea of giving up wanting to be thinner.

At one point, she heard of an opportunity to take a trip to Haiti with a group of volunteers from a local church. They would be helping to rebuild the country after a devastating earthquake. Aisha had always wanted to travel and liked the idea of combining that with helping others; she thought this trip would be a great opportunity, so she signed up to go. She knew she wouldn't be allowed to go if she was sick, so she started taking better care of herself. When she had the urge to not eat, she reminded herself that she had to be in good shape to do the work she was planning to do for others; this thought sometimes helped her put aside the urge and eat in a healthier way. Having the goal of going to Haiti helped Aisha reduce her disordered eating and make positive changes in her life.

Once Aisha got to Haiti, she felt good about herself for reaching her goal in spite of the struggles she had been having. She not only enjoyed her trip and the entire experience but also felt proud of herself for what she had overcome to reach her goal. She also felt really good about the help she was able to provide to people who were less fortunate than she was and about the work her group did while they were there. It was hard work, but it left her feeling like she had really done something worthwhile.

34 Setting Goals for Yourself

Aisha's goal was a big one; obviously not everyone is going to have a goal this grand, especially in the short term. But you can see from her example that setting goals, and reaching them, can have a positive impact in a variety of ways. Now it's your turn to think about how you're doing in this area of your life. Answer the following questions to help you consider your own goals.

What do you see yourself doing in six months? It could be anything from working on managing your emotions in a healthier way to starting college or getting a job or even traveling.

_____
_____
_____

What do you see yourself doing in five years? Don't worry if some of your goals here are repetitive; write them down anyway.

_____
_____
_____

What have you already done to work toward these goals? For example, maybe you've been working with a psychotherapist to help you feel emotionally healthier, working on improving your grades in school, or doing volunteer work to help you get a good job.

What else do you need to work on to reach the goals you listed?

_____
_____
_____

What is one thing you could do today to help you reach one of these goals?

_____

When you're trying to set goals, make sure you break down your bigger, longer-term goals into smaller steps. For example, if one of your goals is to get into a specific college, the smaller, more achievable tasks for you to start working on could include doing volunteer work, working with a tutor once a week to improve your math grade, researching the college online, and talking to people who have been to that school to find out what will increase your chances of acceptance. Getting into the school is the big goal, the end result; breaking this down into smaller steps makes reaching your goal more realistic and achievable and less overwhelming.

What If You Don't Feel Like It?

Many people say that they wish they could do something, but they just don't feel like it; they just don't have the motivation. Many of us seem to have developed the belief that we have to feel motivated before we can do something, but that isn't true. You can adopt a new motto: *Just Do It!* The fact is that we accomplish things all the time that we don't feel that motivated to do. For example, how often do you really feel motivated to do your homework? But (hopefully) you do it anyway! Think about all the other things we manage to get done even when we don't really feel like doing them: getting out of bed in the morning to go to school; going to baseball practice after a long day of classes; meeting with your tutor before you can finally relax after school; getting your chores done around the house; taking care of your younger brother or sister; and so on.

So what makes these things that we do all the time any different from other things that we just can't get ourselves to do? Quite often, it's the thought that we *should* want to do these other things. When it's something we don't want to do, like homework or chores, we do it anyway because we know that we're never really going to feel differently, but when it's something we think we *should* want to do, we think we have to wait until we really want to do it!

The truth is that motivation often doesn't come until after you've started doing an activity. Try treating the activity like a chore and do it regardless of how you feel about it. And you'll usually be surprised to find that after you've started, you feel like doing it and you might even enjoy it. Lisa's story illustrates this point.

> ### Lisa's Story
>
> Lisa had a horse, Bear, whom she boarded at a farm not far from where she lived. She loved her horse, but when she was feeling depressed, she just couldn't get herself motivated to visit him. She would go weeks at a time without even seeing Bear, and this made her feel awful. She kept thinking she should want to go see him, but she just couldn't do it.
>
> Once she actually got out to the barn to see Bear, she ended up not just visiting with him (which was her plan) but also taking him for a ride. They both enjoyed this immensely, and Lisa felt good for accomplishing something very positive that day.

So when you notice yourself thinking *I just don't feel like it*, remember to do it anyway. Strange as this may sound, you might even want to schedule the event for yourself: pull up the calendar on your phone or laptop, or pull out your Day-Timer or agenda, and decide on a day and time you're going to do that particular activity. Make sure it's realistic, and then—here's the hard part—treat the activity as though it were an appointment you've booked or a commitment you've made. There's no canceling unless you're physically ill or something else happens that actually makes it impossible for you to accomplish your goal. This takes the thinking out of the equation and makes it less likely that you'll talk yourself out of doing the activity—if Lisa knows that she has an appointment to go visit Bear on Monday at four o'clock, for example, there's no thinking about whether or not she feels like it; she just goes, because it's booked. Doing things in spite of not feeling like doing them will go a long way toward helping with your painful emotions, as you increase your activity level and the number of positive events you experience in your life.

Seeing the Positive Side

Have you ever noticed that when you feel down, angry, or anxious, or have other painful emotions, all you can think about are the negative things in your life? It's almost like you're wearing blinders that prevent you from seeing anything positive. And often, when there is something positive, you are able to find a way to minimize it so that it still feeds into your negative outlook. For example, when Lisa did get out to see Bear, she would say to herself, *Yeah, I got here to visit him, but he hasn't been ridden in weeks.*

You might have heard the expression "looking at the world through rose-colored glasses," referring to people who have a positive outlook or who are perceived as overly optimistic. Well, the same is true for people who have a negative outlook or are pessimistic—you could say they're wearing dark glasses that tint everything they see.

35 Focusing on the Positive

Your mood obviously has a big impact on the way you see things. When you feel happier, you can see the more positive things in your life for what they are. When you're feeling more down, you tend to focus on the negative. This activity is about taking off those dark glasses and focusing more on the positive things in your life, in spite of how you're feeling.

For the next two weeks, fill out the chart on the following page, noting at least one positive event that happens every single day and your thoughts and emotions about that event. It could be a feeling you experience, something you noticed yourself feeling grateful for, something kind that someone does or says to you—or that you do or say to someone else! It could be a beautiful sunrise, a good mark you get at school, or a peaceful, relaxing time you have as you sit in your backyard with your dog in the sunshine. It doesn't matter what it is; what does matter is that you notice that it's happening.

After you've completed your fourteen days of charting, you might find it helpful to make a point of continuing to notice these positive things as they happen. You can also download this chart at http://www.newharbinger.com/47360 for future use.

Date	Positive Event	Thoughts and Emotions About the Event

Being Mindful to Your Emotions

The dark glasses that prevent us from noticing positive events when we're in a lot of emotional pain can also prevent us from noticing pleasurable emotions that come up. Sometimes this is because the pleasurable emotion is very brief—when you're feeling depressed, angry, or anxious a lot of the time, it's easy to miss the small moments when a pleasant feeling pops up. But it's important to start training yourself to notice when this does happen, so you don't miss out on those times.

Training yourself to be mindful to the positive events that happen throughout your day is one way of doing this—if you're more aware of a positive event, you'll be more aware of the pleasurable emotions that come with it. But have you ever noticed what happens when you've been feeling down a lot and you do happen to notice a pleasurable emotion? Do you tend to think, *Oh great, this is a nice relief from what I've been feeling lately?* Or do you think more along the lines of *Okay, I'd better not get used to this feeling, because it won't last long?*

When we've been experiencing a lot of emotional pain, it's hard for most of us to just accept whatever our emotional experience is, whether it's pleasurable or painful. Instead, when what we feel hurts, we want to avoid it or push it away; and when it's a pleasurable feeling, we want to cling to it and try to stop it from ending. Trying to get rid of or hold on to emotions this way usually makes those same emotions hang around when we don't want them and disappear when we do want them. In chapter 4, we talked about how accepting a situation will help reduce your suffering; the same holds true with your emotions. When you can fully accept that you feel anxious, your anxiety will become more tolerable and gradually fade. When you can fully accept that in this moment you feel content—rather than worrying about when it might end or trying to figure out a way to continue feeling this way—you will enjoy it more and the feeling will linger.

36 Being Mindful to Your Emotions

This activity will help you get the hang of being mindful to your emotion, regardless of how good or bad the emotion feels. Sitting down in a comfortable position, just begin to notice what you're feeling. Thoughts will likely come into your awareness, and you might notice certain physical sensations. Whatever comes into your awareness, just notice it: allow yourself to sense it and to label it without judging it. For example, you might notice that you have butterflies in your stomach—don't judge it, try to interpret it, or think about what it might mean; just note *butterflies in my stomach*. You might notice that you're having worried thoughts about a situation in your life. Again, just notice this without judgment, and label it (for example, *I'm having worried thoughts about my exam next week*). When you notice a feeling you're experiencing, do the same thing. Without judging it, trying to push it away or change it in some way, just observe it and describe it to yourself: *I'm feeling anxious*. It can also help if you repeat the name of the emotion to yourself three or four times, for example, *anxiety ... anxiety ... anxiety*. By doing this, you're acknowledging the emotion without trying to do anything about it. And with this self-validation, when you can fully accept an emotional experience, it becomes less painful (see chapter 4). This also holds true when you expect to feel something that you don't feel, and judge yourself for this—for example, have you ever thought to yourself, *This is a happy moment, why am I not more excited?* Judging yourself for not feeling something also causes emotional pain, so practice accepting what is there and what isn't. This exercise can also be helpful with emotions that aren't painful. Notice what you're feeling, and acknowledge it, for example, *contentment ... contentment ... contentment.*

By acknowledging your emotions in this way, you can move away from the tendency to judge them, try to cling to the ones you want to keep, or push away the ones you don't want to have. Instead, you just experience whatever emotion is present in this moment.

Wrapping Up

In this chapter you've learned about how to increase the pleasurable emotions in your life. We looked at increasing the number of activities that you do for pleasure as well as activities that create feelings of accomplishment and pride. We also discussed the importance of doing things even when you don't necessarily feel like doing them and of setting long- and short-term goals for yourself. Finally, we looked at the importance of being mindful to your emotions—how noticing them and accepting them can help keep the painful emotions from sticking around and the pleasurable ones from departing.

In the next chapter we'll look at how you can make positive changes in relationships, which will both contribute to feelings of pleasure and increase your ability to manage your emotions more effectively.

CHAPTER SEVEN

Improving Your Relationships

Relationships are a big part of our lives, and they can affect our moods. When things are going well in our relationships, we feel happier; when things aren't so great, they can bring us down. We need to have friends, family, people who support us and care about us, and people with whom we can socialize and do activities. Having these kinds of relationships helps us to be more emotionally healthy; unfortunately, though, relationships can also get quite complicated.

In this chapter, you'll first think about whether you have enough satisfying relationships in your life and whether you need to consider ending some relationships that aren't healthy. Then you'll learn some skills that will help you improve the relationships you have in your life. But first, let's start by looking at an example of why it's so important to have relationships in your life.

Zack's Story

Zack was twelve when the kids at school started to bully him. He wasn't sure why they started picking on him, but they were relentless. The people he used to hang out with no longer wanted to be friends with him, so Zack was very isolated and lonely at school, which really got him down. He began to feel depressed on a regular basis, to the point that he sometimes thought about killing himself.

Fortunately, one of the guidance counselors at school saw what was happening with Zack and noticed the steady drop in his mood. She made sure she had regular contact with Zack so that he knew he wasn't alone and could go to the guidance office whenever he was having troubles. She also let Zack's parents know what was going on, and together they got Zack involved with a support group for kids who were being bullied. Zack was able to make some friends in that group, where he felt more accepted and understood, and this helped him start to feel better about himself again. The bullying finally stopped because Zack's parents got involved, but things remained hard at school because some kids still didn't want to be friends with him. In spite of this, Zack knew he had other friends now, and he looked forward to spending time with them outside of school.

Relationships are incredibly important in our lives. Without them, we feel alone and isolated; we have no one to share our pain or our successes with, and this can lead to intense feelings of sadness and loneliness. Loneliness, by the way, can not only cause emotional difficulties like the ones we've been talking about but also have consequences on our physical health. One study actually showed that loneliness and social isolation can be as damaging to our physical health as smoking fifteen cigarettes a day (Holt-Lunstad et al. 2015).

37 Thinking About Your Current Relationships

For each of the following areas, think hard about who in your life meets these specific needs, and write down their names. You might find that people overlap in some areas, and that's okay; just make sure you're as thorough as possible, so you get an accurate idea of which areas you might need to work on strengthening. If you need more room, use another piece of paper.

Family support

Do you have certain family members with whom you are close—people you feel comfortable confiding in, who understand you, and on whom you know you can count for support? These might also be people you consider as family even though they are not actually biological relatives.

_____
_____
_____

Close friends

Do you have a best friend or friends you know you can count on, who will support you and stick by you? They don't have to be people your own age; you may have someone older or younger whom you think about in this way. The important thing is, you know they care about you and will help you through hard times.

_____
_____
_____

People you look up to

Is there anyone in your life you look up to, someone you think of as a positive influence, someone you really respect, who in turn is supportive of and respectful toward you? This could be a teacher, a coach, a leader in the community, someone you know through your religious affiliation, and so on.

_____ _____
_____ _____
_____ _____

People you socialize with

You might find that you have some friends you do social things with but don't really think of as close friends with whom you would share personal information. They might be fun to hang out with, but you don't count them among your good friends in whom you would confide.

_____ _____
_____ _____
_____ _____

Unhealthy relationships

Can you think of any relationships you have that are unhealthy in some way? For example, maybe someone who used to be a good friend now drinks a lot, uses drugs, or engages in other behaviors you don't agree with, and you're not sure what to do about it. Or perhaps there's someone you'd like to be close with but who doesn't treat you very well. Think about any of these relationships that feel unhealthy or unsatisfying to you, and write the names of those people here:

_____ _____
_____ _____

Now think about what this exercise was like for you. Was it difficult or fairly easy? Did it bring up any emotions for you? Looking at what you wrote in each of the earlier categories, what does it tell you about the relationships you have in your life: Do you have enough relationships, and are you satisfied with those you do have? Do you need more people in certain areas of your life? Maybe you have many people to hang out with but not enough close friends. Perhaps you have relationships that need more attention to make them healthy and satisfying again. Write down anything that came up for you:

_____
_____
_____
_____
_____
_____

The rest of this chapter will help you look at ways to develop new relationships, if you believe you need more of these in your life. We'll also look at skills that will help you be more effective with other people so that you have healthy, satisfying relationships. As you read on, keep in mind what you wrote in the previous activity, thinking about what goals you might set for your relationships.

Bringing More Relationships into Your Life

You might have noticed that you have a tendency to isolate yourself when you're feeling especially emotional, cutting yourself off from your friends and other people who care about you. Or, if you're feeling angry a lot and have been expressing that anger in unhealthy ways (like lashing out at your friends), you might find that your friends want to spend less time around you. This will have the same effect—you end up isolated, by yourself more often, with fewer people in your life. If you've found yourself feeling like you don't have enough people in your life, what can you do about it?

First, you can consider whether you can salvage friendships you used to have. Maybe you had a fight with or drifted away from a really good friend, and the relationship ended. If this was an important relationship for you, and you regret its ending, perhaps you could reach out to that person. Keep in mind that this person might not be interested or that the relationship might not be the same as it was before, but if it's a relationship you'd like to restart, then it's worth trying.

Second, you can look at the relationships you already have and see if there are some you can develop into something more—like Carlos did.

> ### Carlos's Story
>
> Carlos played soccer every summer. A few of the people from his team went to his high school, and they were always pleasant when he saw them, but they had never been his friends. Carlos decided he would try to get to know them better. So one day, rather than eating lunch in the cafeteria by himself as he usually did, he found two of the people from his soccer team at a table and asked if he could join them. This became a regular thing, and they seemed quite happy to have Carlos eat with them. Soon they were not just having lunch but sometimes walking home after school together, and they found they had interests in common other than soccer. Slowly, these two acquaintances became Carlos's friends.

Third, you can think of ways to meet new people. This can be a scary idea, especially if anxiety is a factor for you. But remember that having healthy relationships is one way of increasing the pleasurable emotions in your life, so this is very important.

38 Increasing the Relationships in Your Life

This activity will help you look at different ways to bring more relationships into your life and how to improve in these areas. I would suggest doing this exercise even if you think you have enough friends in your life; you can never have too many friends!

Rekindling past relationships

First, think about some people from your past with whom you'd like to reconnect. Write down the names of everyone who pops into your head:

_____

_____

Choose one person who stands out for you: how could you go about getting back in touch with that person? It might be easy if she still goes to your school or you still have her phone number, but what if she moved and you're not sure where she is? Write down some thoughts about how you could get in touch (for example, see if you can find her on Snapchat or Instagram, and send a short message to say hello):

Next, consider what you would say when you do make contact. For example, do you need to clear the air about something that happened between you? Maybe you were lashing out at your friend, because you were angry about other things, and she got tired of it; you might need to explain that you realize your anger is a problem and have been working on it. Perhaps an apology is needed. Maybe your life has been controlled by anxiety, and this led to cutting a lot of people out of your life. Do you need to explain this so that your friend knows it's not likely to happen again? Write down some thoughts about what you might say:

_____

_____

Of course, the next step is to get in touch with this person and see if you can start working on becoming friends again. Remember that the relationship likely won't be the same as it was before, especially in the beginning; friendships take time to develop, so have patience. And if you don't get a response, remember you have skills now to help you with that—maybe you'll need to practice accepting this reality, act opposite to a strong emotion that arises, or use some self-soothing to help you get through some difficult moments.

Changing current relationships into something more

Now think about some people currently in your life whom you'd like to get to know better. Perhaps, like Carlos, you play a sport and would like to become better friends with some of your teammates. Or maybe you have a part-time job or do volunteer work and have met someone with whom you'd like to spend more time. Write down the names of any people you can think of and any other thoughts about this:

_____

_____

How can you start to develop this friendship (for example, sitting with someone different at lunch or asking your coworker to go for a break with you)?

_____

_____

Finding ways to meet new people

Now for the really tough part: can you think of how you could go about meeting some new people? Add your ideas to these examples:

Join a group on meetup.com.	Get involved with a community youth group.
Join a new club at school.	Volunteer at a food bank or animal shelter.
Sign up for Spanish lessons.	Try out for a sport at school.
_____	_____
_____	_____

For many of us, the idea of going out and meeting new people is extremely intimidating. Keep in mind, though, that relationships are a necessary part of life. If this is really scary for you, consider whether there is someone you could do this with. Maybe you know someone in a similar situation, and together you can work on increasing the relationships in your lives.

Also, it can be helpful if you think about a time in your life when you had more relationships: people you could call to talk about things; someone you knew who would always be there for you; people you could call to just hang out. Do you remember what it felt like to be accepted, to be a part of a group (even a small one), to feel understood and liked by others? Human beings are social; we need relationships in our lives. So, as difficult as it may be, you need to find ways of filling this need.

How Effective Communication Helps Relationships

Many of the skills you've already learned in this workbook can help you have healthy relationships. For example, improving your self-awareness and ability to manage yourself through mindfulness and the other skills you've learned—as well as what you've learned about emotions, the purpose they serve and how they affect you—will help you be more effective in your relationships. Using skills to not act on urges that would make a crisis situation worse helps prevent others from getting burned out and frustrated with you, which also has a positive impact on your relationships. In this section, we're going to look at some specific skills that can help you communicate better with people. These skills will help you keep and even improve your relationships with others.

Have you ever found yourself feeling hurt, disappointed, or angry with a friend and not wanting to talk to your friend about it because you're fearful that saying how you feel would just make things worse? Perhaps you worry that the other person will get angry with you in return and maybe stop being your friend altogether. So you decide not to have that conversation, and you stuff your feelings down, or you decide the friendship isn't worth the emotional pain you're experiencing, so you plan to end the relationship. There are lots of things that can go wrong with a relationship when we're not communicating properly. Let's take a look at some examples of how we communicate.

Passive

If you are a *passive* person, you often stuff your emotions instead of expressing them. This is usually because of fear—maybe you're afraid you'll hurt the other person, or he'll get angry with you and not want to be your friend anymore. It feels easier to just sit on your emotions and not say anything rather than to speak up and risk having the other person think or feel anything negative toward you. This is understandable; many people fear conflict, and of course we don't want to lose relationships. But being passive often results in others hurting you and violating your rights. It also shows a lack of respect for your own needs, and over time this will have negative consequences for you and for your relationships; you'll start to feel resentful toward the other person because you're not getting your needs met. In other words, it's not effective.

Aggressive

If you're an *aggressive* person, you express yourself in a dominating and controlling way—you might yell, swear, throw things, threaten, and so on. You're concerned with getting your own way, regardless of how it affects others. Bullies are aggressive communicators; they're direct in a forceful, demanding way. When you communicate in this way, you usually leave others feeling resentful, hurt, and even afraid of you. You might get your way, but it's at the expense of others. This style of communicating might also come at an expense to you, if you end up feeling guilty or ashamed for the way you behaved. Being aggressive also makes it more likely that you'll lose relationships that are important to you, because others usually won't put up with being disrespected and mistreated for very long.

Passive-Aggressive

If you're *passive-aggressive,* you usually don't express yourself directly, again because of fear (for example, fear of conflict or fear of how the other person will react). People who are passive-aggressive express their emotions in more subtle ways: using sarcasm, giving others the silent treatment, slamming a door as they leave a room. If you are passive-aggressive, you can certainly get your message across without actually saying the words, but you do it in a way that's still damaging to the relationship. Or you may be indirect and unclear with your message—you say one thing but then send a contradictory message (for example, you say, "It doesn't matter," if your friends don't choose the movie you wanted to see, but then you stay quiet for the rest of the night because you're angry about the choice).

Assertive

Being *assertive* is the healthiest form of communication. When you're assertive, you express your thoughts, feelings, and opinions in a clear, honest, and appropriate way. You're respectful toward the other person and toward yourself. While you're concerned with trying to get your own needs met, you also try to meet the needs of the other person as much as possible. Assertiveness also means listening and negotiating so that others choose to cooperate willingly with you, because they, too, are getting something out of the interaction (Van Dijk 2009). When you communicate this way with others, they will feel respected and valued, and they'll be more likely to respond by treating you the same way.

People who feel good about themselves tend to communicate assertively. When you have healthy self-esteem, you recognize your right to express your beliefs and feelings. But it works the other way around too—by communicating assertively, you improve how you feel about yourself. Being assertive will improve your interactions with others and your relationships overall, which will also help you feel good about yourself.

Keep in mind that it takes time and practice to change your patterns, so it might be difficult for you to become assertive right away if this isn't how you're used to communicating.

39 What's Your Communication Style?

Before you can change a pattern, you first have to be aware of what it is. Read the following statements to help you get an idea of what your own communication style is. You'll likely see that you behave in many of these ways at different times, so when you're thinking about each statement, place a check mark next to those that seem to describe you best. When you've finished, add up the number of check marks in each section to see which communication styles you use most often.

Passive

☐ I try to push my feelings away rather than express them to others.

☐ I worry that expressing myself will cause others to be angry with me or to not like me.

☐ I often hear myself saying "I don't care" or "It doesn't matter to me" when I do care, and it actually does matter.

☐ I try not to "rock the boat," keeping quiet because I don't want to upset others.

☐ I often go along with others' opinions because I don't want to be different.
Total: _____

Aggressive

☐ I am concerned with getting my own way, regardless of how it affects others.
☐ I often yell, swear, or use other aggressive means of communicating.
☐ My friends are often afraid of me.
☐ I don't really care if others get what they need as long as my needs are met.
☐ I've heard others say that I have an "It's my way or the highway" attitude.
Total: _____

Passive-Aggressive

☐ I have a tendency to be sarcastic in conversations with others as a way of indirectly expressing an emotion or opinion.
☐ I tend to give people the silent treatment when I'm angry with them.
☐ I often find myself saying one thing but really thinking another.
☐ I'm generally reluctant to express my emotions in words, resorting instead to aggressive behaviors, like slamming doors.

☐ I try to get my message across in more subtle ways for fear that expressing myself will cause others to be angry with me or to stop liking me.
Total: _____

Assertive

☐ I believe that I have the right to express my opinions and emotions.

☐ When I'm having a disagreement with someone, I can express my opinions and emotions clearly and honestly.

☐ In communicating with others, I treat them with respect while also respecting myself.

☐ I listen closely to what other people are saying, sending the message that I'm trying to understand their perspective.

☐ I try to negotiate with the other person if we have different goals rather than just focus on getting my own needs met.
Total: _____

Now take a look to see if you scored higher in one area. You might find that you tend to use the same communication style in different situations, or you might notice that you have traits of some or all of the styles, depending on the situation and the person you're communicating with.

It's important to be aware of your own patterns so that you can work on becoming more assertive. And even if you're already being assertive on a regular basis, take the time to read the following skills to help you continue to do well; it's difficult to be assertive all the time with everyone in our lives!

How to Communicate Assertively

Hopefully you now see that being assertive will help you in your relationships. But how do you do it? The guidelines that follow can help.

Be Clear About What You Want

Assertiveness is about asking someone for something, such as asking your dad for a ride to the mall, asking a teacher for help with an assignment, or asking a friend to go to the movies on the weekend. Assertiveness can also be about saying no to someone else's request—like when a friend asks you to loan her some money and you don't want to because she hasn't repaid you in the past. The first thing you need to do, to communicate assertively, is to decide exactly what you want in a situation.

Once you've decided on what you'd like the outcome to be, then clearly, honestly, and specifically say what it is you want to say. For example, if you're feeling hurt or angered by something the other person did, tell him specifically what it was he did and how you feel about it. When you're doing this, try to state your own feelings first: saying, "I felt hurt when you said this" rather than "When you said this, I felt hurt." It might not seem like much of a difference, but the first way comes across as you taking responsibility for your own emotions while the second seems to blame the other person for how you feel.

This is an important idea to remember—that we are each responsible for our own emotions. You don't want to blame others for how you feel any more than you want them blaming you for how they feel. Let's look at an example to help clarify this.

Margarita's Story

Margarita was home from boarding school for spring break. She would be home for only a short time and was trying to get in as much visiting time as she could with her family and friends. She spent two days with her sister and her sister's family, and they had talked about her returning there for another two days before she went back to school. As that time approached, however, Margarita decided she wouldn't return to her sister's, after all, because she still had a few friends she hadn't seen. Margarita texted her sister, explaining her decision. But the message she got back told Margarita how sad and disappointed her

> sister was and that her niece and nephew were also very disappointed that they wouldn't get to see Aunt Margarita again for a long time.

Although it was Margarita's decision that led to her sister feeling sad and disappointed, it was neither Margarita's fault that her sister felt that way nor Margarita's responsibility to make her sister feel better by changing her decision. Margarita could decide from her wise self to change her mind, after realizing how her sister, niece, and nephew felt, and, of course, it would make sense for her to do that! But the point is, other people are not always going to agree with the choices you make. How they feel is their responsibility, not yours, and you're not obligated to change your mind because of how someone else reacts to your decision.

Listen Mindfully

Remember that being assertive isn't just about getting your own needs met but also about trying to meet the needs of the other person so that you both come away satisfied. To accomplish this, it's important to know what the other person wants from the interaction. So pay attention, and make sure you're not doing something else while you're talking; texting someone or having your earbuds in will make the other person feel like you're not really paying attention and you don't care about what's being said. Instead, listen mindfully—with your full attention, noticing when your mind wanders and bringing it back to the present moment.

Be Nonjudgmental

In chapter 4, we looked at the importance of being nonjudgmental to reduce the amount of emotional pain you experience. This skill is also incredibly helpful when it comes to relationships. You know how it feels when you're being judged, so try to talk to the other person the way you would like to be spoken to. Don't blame, don't judge—just stick to the facts and how you feel about a situation.

Validate Others

Validating others also comes in handy when you're trying to communicate effectively. Don't interrupt: giving others room to talk indicates that what they're saying is important to you. Reflect back to others what they say to you, so it's clear you're listening and understand what they're saying; if necessary, ask questions to clarify so that you do understand. Let them know that what they have to say is important to you and that it makes sense, even if you don't agree with it. We've all had the experience at some point of being validated by another person, and we know how good it feels to be heard and understood. Doing the same for your friends will go a long way toward improving your relationships.

Act According to Your Values

When you're asserting yourself, it's important to know what your values are (if you need to, review the work you did on this in chapter 1) and to stick to them (Linehan 1993). If someone asks you to do something that goes against what you believe in, you probably won't feel good about yourself if you agree to the request. For example, your friend tells you she's going to a party this weekend, and she's going to tell her parents that she's sleeping over at your house, so she asks you to lie to her parents if they call your house looking for her. If lying goes against your values, you probably won't feel good about yourself—or about your relationship with this friend—if you agree to her request.

Making excuses also falls in this category. For example, have you ever had an urge to make up an excuse when someone asks you to do something that you really don't want to do? It's perfectly okay to say no and to be honest about the reason—even if it's just because you don't want to! Also important to note is that you don't have to provide a reason—you can just say no. If you can be assertive and say that you don't want to do what the person is asking of you, your self-respect will increase (Van Dijk

2009). Of course, you also have to balance this with not damaging the relationship. Telling your friend that you don't feel good about lying to her parents is one thing; telling your friend that you don't want to come over to her house because you don't like her parents is another! When the truth would be hurtful, it's okay to resort to the *little white lie* (a harmless or inconsequential lie). Not being entirely truthful, however, should come from a place of internal wisdom rather than from your emotional self; and doing this infrequently and with caution will ensure that it doesn't affect your self-respect.

Don't Overapologize

One last word here about self-respect: don't overdo it with "I'm sorry." Often we have an urge to apologize for things that aren't actually our fault. Saying you're sorry means that you're taking responsibility for something, that is, acknowledging you feel like you're in the wrong and will indicate that to others as well. Over time, this feeling of being responsible for things that you're really not responsible for will decrease your self-respect. So apologize only when you've done something you truly need to apologize for (Linehan 1993). You can also consider other words that might fit better than an apology—when you bump into someone walking down the busy hallway at school, how about "Excuse me" rather than "I'm sorry"?

40 Reflecting on Your Assertiveness Skills

Now that you've learned about some specific techniques that will help you be more assertive, take a moment to think about what skills you use already and the areas you need to work on. Following is the list of skills just reviewed; in the space provided, make some notes about how you do with each skill; for example, do you often use this technique, can you identify situations or people with whom you have a hard time using it, and so on?

Be clear about what you want. Do you clearly and honestly express your opinions and emotions?

_____
_____
_____

Listen mindfully. Do you set aside everything else and focus just on the person you're interacting with?

_____
_____

Be nonjudgmental. Do you try to stay away from judgments and blaming and just stick to the facts and your emotions?

Validate others. Do you give the other person space to talk, uninterrupted? Do you reflect back what the other person is saying and ask questions to make sure you understand?

Act according to your values. Do you say no to requests that go against your values? Do you try to be honest and stay away from making excuses?

Don't overapologize. Do you often hear yourself apologizing for things that aren't your fault?

Finding Balance in Relationships

You've probably heard before that balance is important in relationships, that there has to be give and take. Now that you've given some thought to how you communicate and what you can do to improve your communication skills, we're going to look at one last, very important area: finding that balance.

Priorities vs. Responsibilities

First, it's important to look at exactly what it is you're balancing. In chapter 6, you learned about the importance of having activities in your life that are pleasurable: maybe fun, interesting, relaxing, or fulfilling. Think of these as your *priorities*. It's a priority for you to do them because you enjoy them or they're important to you for some other reason. For example, learning Spanish might not exactly be fun for you, but it's important to you because you plan to travel a lot or you want to get a job overseas when you're older.

Of course, we all have certain *responsibilities* as well—those expectations that others have of us, whether it's going to school, doing homework, doing chores, or taking care of younger siblings. We've already talked about the importance of having priorities, but what about responsibilities? The truth is, it's important to have responsibilities too, in order to feel needed or fulfilled. As much as we sometimes complain about our responsibilities, without them we just wouldn't have enough in our lives (Linehan 1993).

Some things can be both priorities and responsibilities. For example, going to school is a responsibility. Legally you have to go, and your parents insist that you do. But maybe you really like school, or maybe you tolerate it because you want to go to college or get your dream job as a pilot; if that's the case, school is also a priority for you. Another good example is walking your dog—it's a responsibility, a demand that is put on you by your dog and perhaps by your parents, but if you also really enjoy spending that time with your pet, it's both a priority *and* a responsibility. The goal, as with most things in a healthy life, is to look at *balancing* our enjoyable activities with our responsibilities.

Quite often we run into problems in relationships when our priorities conflict with our responsibilities or the demands that others put on us (Linehan 1993). For example, your mom tells you that this Tuesday she'll be getting home from work late because of a meeting, and you'll need to get your little sister from the school-bus stop, but tryouts for the cheerleading team are also on Tuesday. This conflict is the perfect time to use your assertiveness skills. Yelling at your mom is not going to work. Nodding your head and hiding your tears is not going to work. Going to your room and slamming the door is not going to work. You need to clearly and honestly express to your mom the facts of the situation and how you feel about it, and see if you can negotiate a solution that can meet both your needs.

41 Assertiveness Practice

Now it's time to think about putting these assertiveness skills into practice. Think of a past situation in which you could have been more assertive; perhaps you can think of a time when your priority conflicted with something that someone else wanted you to do. Write down some details about the situation; for example, who was involved and what was the problem?

_____
_____

What did you actually say in the situation? What was the outcome?

_____
_____

What could you have done or said differently to create a better outcome for yourself and the other person?

_____
_____

Think about a situation that is likely to happen in the future; for example, maybe someone will ask you to do something that you don't want to do, or there's a party coming up that you haven't yet asked your parents about. Write about the situation here:

_____

_____

How could you handle this situation assertively? Get specific here: write down the actual words you would want to say to the other person. Also make sure you're being clear about what it is that you want from the other person, whether there's something you're asking for or you want to say no to something they're requesting of you. The clearer and more specific you can be, the more likely you'll reach your goal.

_____

_____

After you've had this conversation, come back to this workbook and write some notes about how you did. Did you act assertively? What was the outcome? Were you happy with the results? Were there things you could have done differently to bring about a more positive outcome?

Now take some time to consider a conversation you need to have with someone—this could be asking your teacher for some extra help in chemistry; asking your parents if you can borrow the car this weekend; or even asking someone at your cell phone company for help with reducing your monthly bill. Imagining these conversations ahead of time will make getting your needs met much more likely, so write out what you would like to say using the assertiveness skills you've learned.

_____
_____
_____
_____
_____

Now practice. Read your words to yourself in a mirror, so you can see your how you look while you say these words. Practice having this conversation with a trusted person if you can to build your confidence. Make sure you envision yourself clearly saying what you want to say. Practicing a positive outcome, even though it's in your imagination, actually does make it more likely that you'll get your needs met!

Wrapping Up

In this chapter, we've looked at a lot of information to help you with relationships. You learned about why relationships are so important and why we need them, and you've gained some tips to help you increase the number of relationships in your life. You've learned about how effective communication can go a long way toward improving your relationships and also learned about the different communication styles and how to be more assertive.

Remember that our relationships influence how we feel emotionally, so it's important to have positive, healthy people in our lives. We're almost at the end of this workbook, so make sure you're continuing to give a lot of thought to these skills.

CHAPTER EIGHT

Putting It All Together

You've learned a lot of different skills throughout this book that can help you reduce your emotional load and manage your emotions more effectively. Hopefully, you've been working hard on putting these skills into practice, and you've seen some changes—even though they might only be small ones right now. The longer you continue practicing the skills you've learned here, the more positive changes you'll see. In this chapter, we're going to take a quick look at how you've done so far and where you need to go from here, and then you'll learn one final skill to help you get there.

42 Self-Assessment

This is the same self-assessment you completed in the introduction to this workbook. Take a few minutes now to complete it once again, by checking off each of the following statements that apply to you, and see if you've been able to make some changes in your life with the new skills you've learned.

Mindfulness

☐ I often say or do things without thinking and later regret my words or actions.

☐ I usually feel like I don't really know who I am, what I like and dislike, and what my values are.

☐ I often go along with the beliefs and values of others so that I won't feel different.

☐ I sometimes feel bad or upset without knowing exactly what I'm feeling or why.

☐ I often judge myself or other people critically.

☐ I frequently try to avoid things that make me uncomfortable.

☐ I often find myself saying things like "This shouldn't have happened," "It's not fair," or "It's not right."

Emotion Regulation

☐ I try to avoid my emotions by sleeping, partying a lot, immersing myself in video games, or doing other things that take me away from my feelings.

☐ Emotions are scary for me. I try to push them away or get rid of them in other ways.

☐ I tend to dwell on the things I don't like about my life.

☐ I am not very active and don't regularly do activities that I enjoy.

☐ I neglect setting short- or long-term goals for myself; for example, I avoid thinking about where I'd like to be in a year, in two years, or in five years.

☐ I often don't have events or situations coming up in my life to look forward to.

Distress Tolerance

☐ I regularly dwell on painful things that have happened to me.

☐ I often find myself having painful emotions because I think about things that have happened in the past or that might happen in the future.

☐ I tend to ignore my own needs; for example, I don't usually take the time to do things that are relaxing, soothing, or enjoyable for me.

☐ When I'm in crisis, I often find myself making the situation worse by doing problematic things like drinking or using drugs, lashing out at others who are trying to help, and so on.

☐ I tend to lose friends or the support of my family because they don't like the things I do to cope with my emotions.

Interpersonal Effectiveness

☐ I feel like I give or take more in my relationships rather than having a balance of give *and* take.

☐ I often feel taken advantage of in relationships.

☐ When relationships aren't going well, I tend to end them without first trying to fix the problems.

☐ I often struggle to keep relationships in my life.

☐ I tend to be more passive in communicating with others; for example, I don't stick up for myself or I go along with the other person all the time.

☐ I tend to be more aggressive in communication with others; for example, I try to force my opinion on the other person.

☐ I tend to get into relationships with others who do unhealthy things, like use drugs or drink a lot, or who get into a lot of trouble with their parents or even with the police, or with people who don't treat me well or who bully me.

Compare your first assessment to this one. Do you notice any differences? Have you started to work toward some of the goals you identified at the beginning of the book? On the following scale, rate where you think you are in terms of having made positive changes in your life:

```
0     1     2     3     4     5     6     7     8     9     10
No change              Some change                    Big change
```

Write about any of the changes you've noticed:

Maybe you noticed that you haven't made any changes—if so, do your best to not judge yourself! If you haven't made changes, why do you think that is? Have things gotten in the way of your using skills? Have you been using skills and still not seen any changes yet? Write about your thoughts:

Take some time now to consider what you could do differently to help you make changes. For example, you might need to work your way through this book a second time, going more slowly, practicing the skills more as you go along. Sometimes people read through books like this too quickly, without putting enough effort into practice; as a result, they don't absorb the material thoroughly enough to incorporate the skills into their lives. Going through this workbook too quickly can also cause you to feel overwhelmed by the number of skills presented. Take it one step at a time. Even if you have to spend a couple of months just focusing on one skill, that's okay: do what you need to do to learn the material and make helpful and healthy changes in your life.

Sometimes people have learning disabilities or other problems, such as attention deficit disorder (ADD) or attention deficit/hyperactivity disorder (ADHD), that make it harder to learn. If this is the case for you, enlist the help of someone you trust to act as a kind of tutor, just like you would for your schoolwork. Maybe you need to work through this book during the summer, when you don't have classes, so that you can focus more on the material and not get overwhelmed. The bottom line is, do whatever you need to do to help yourself learn these skills and make them part of your life. Make some notes here about what you need to do to help yourself in this way. I've provided some examples to help you get started:

- I need to start at the beginning of the book, really think about what my goals are, write them down, and then focus on the skills that will help most with those goals.
- I can post reminders to myself (like sticky notes or notes in my cell phone), so I won't forget to use the skills.
- I can tell my parents the specific skill I'm working on and get them to read the workbook with me so that we can talk about the skill and they can help me remember to practice it.

Keeping an Open Mind

One other thing can get in the way of people making these kinds of changes in their lives: they shut down the possibility of changing. We've all had this experience—you know there's something you could do that would be helpful, but you just can't be bothered. It feels like it takes too much energy or thought. You don't have the time. You're too tired. You have too many other things to do. It's not fair that you got stuck with this problem, so forget it; you're just going to ignore it and maybe it'll go away on its own.

The problem is, it won't go away on its own. You can ignore it all you want, and that just makes it worse. When you shut down the possibility of making changes, you're being *willful* (May 1982). Instead of trying, you're closing yourself off from possibilities, from change, from your friends, family, and the universe. You're disconnecting. Willfulness is about giving up, about sitting on your hands and not trying to do anything to help yourself.

The opposite of being willful is being willing. Willingness is opening yourself up to possibilities, to change. It's unfolding your arms and saying "Okay, I'll give it a try" and doing the best you can with what you have. It's saying yes to the universe.

Dr. Linehan (1993) uses the analogy of playing cards. In a card game, you have to play the cards you're dealt. Being willful would be refusing to play your cards, saying "Forget it," "I quit," or "Whatever, I don't care." Willfulness is also when you try to cheat by stealing a card from the deck or looking at your opponent's hand. Being willing, on the other hand, would be playing your cards, acknowledging that maybe they're not the best cards but that you're going to do your best with what you've been dealt.

What to Do with Willfulness

So what do you do when you're feeling willful—when you see yourself shutting down, refusing to try to do anything to make your life better? Just acknowledge it. Accept it. Notice that it's happening. Say to yourself, *Oh, wait a second. I think I'm feeling willful right now.* Then do your best to turn to willingness. Pull out this workbook and see if you can find a skill that might help: doing a forward bend, doing some paced breathing, and opening up your posture (unfolding your arms, unclenching your fists, and doing your best to loosen up any tight muscles) are all examples of skills that can help you get to a more willing place. If you're in a crisis, pull out your crisis plan and follow it to get through the crisis without making it worse.

43 Your Experience of Willfulness and Willingness

As noted before, you can't change something until you recognize what's happening. In this exercise, you'll start to think about how you think, feel, and act when you're feeling both willful and willing.

Ways I'm willful

Think about a time when you were willful, or come back to this exercise after you've experienced willfulness. Write about what this experience was like for you. What kinds of thoughts did you have? (Remember, willful thoughts are often thoughts of giving up, of not trying.) What emotions came up for you? (Hint: they'll be painful emotions, often of anger, frustration, bitterness, and so on.) How did you behave? (Examples of willful behavior include yelling and swearing at others; threatening suicide; using drugs, alcohol, or another means of escape; or harming yourself in some way.)

Ways I'm willing

Now think about a time when you were willing, when things were difficult but you did your best with what you had. Write about what this experience was like for you. What kinds of thoughts did you have? (They'll likely be encouraging and validating thoughts, like *It's hard, but I have to keep trying anyway.*) What emotions came up for you? (Hint: the pain won't necessarily have gone away, but you might also have felt hopeful or proud of yourself for trying even when things were tough.) How did you behave? (These would be healthy, helpful behaviors like asking someone for help or using skills you've learned to cope.)

Wrapping Up

Willingness is a major factor in your ability to improve your life using the skills you've learned, both in this book and elsewhere. You can read all you want or go to therapy every week, but until you become aware of when willfulness has arisen in you, and until you can let go of it and turn your mind to being willing, nothing in your life will change. You might have heard the saying "You can lead a horse to water, but you can't make it drink." You've been given these skills, but no one can make you practice them. Only you can do that. So what do you think? Are you willing?

Answers

Activity 2

1. Mindful; 2. Unmindful; 3. Unmindful; 4. Mindful; 5. Unmindful; 6. Mindful

Activity 9

1. Anger—Kayla could tell Mary she wants her to be less critical of her.
2. Anxiety—Joshua could talk to Emily about his concern that she hasn't been keeping in touch.
3. Sadness—Nicole could talk to Samantha to see if they can resolve their differences.
4. Guilt—Matt could admit to his mom that he took her cell phone and face the consequences.

Activity 10

1. Thought; 2. Emotion; 3. Thought; 4. Behavior; 5. Behavior; 6. Thought; 7. Emotion; 8. Behavior; 9. Emotion; 10. Behavior; 11. Thought; 12. Emotion

Activity 13

1. Wise Self; 2. Reasoning Self; 3. Emotional Self; 4. Wise Self; 5. Reasoning Self;

6. Emotional Self

Activity 18

1. Judgment; 2. Judgment; 3. Judgment; 4. Nonjudgment; 5. Nonjudgment; 6. Judgment; 7. Nonjudgment; 8. Nonjudgment; 9. Judgment; 10. Nonjudgment

Additional Reading

Resources for Depression

Copeland, Mary Ellen, and Stuart Copans. 2002. *Recovering from Depression: A Workbook for Teens.* Revised edition. Baltimore: Brooks Publishing.

Schab, Lisa. 2008. *Beyond the Blues: A Workbook to Help Teens Overcome Depression.* Oakland, CA: New Harbinger Publications.

Resources for Bipolar Disorder

Van Dijk, Sheri. 2009. *The Dialectical Behavior Therapy Skills Workbook for Bipolar Disorder: Using DBT to Regain Control of Your Emotions and Your Life.* Oakland, CA: New Harbinger Publications.

Van Dijk, Sheri, and Karma Guindon. 2010. *The Bipolar Workbook for Teens: DBT Skills to Help You Control Mood Swings.* Oakland, CA: New Harbinger Publications.

Resources for Anxiety

Antony, Martin, and Richard Swinson. 2000. *The Shyness and Social Anxiety Workbook: Proven, Step-by-Step Techniques for Overcoming Your Fear.* Oakland, CA: New Harbinger Publications.

———. 2009. *When Perfect Isn't Good Enough: Strategies for Coping with Perfectionism.* Oakland, CA: New Harbinger Publications.

Burns, David D. 2007. *When Panic Attacks: The New, Drug-Free Anxiety Therapy That Can Change Your Life.* New York: Broadway Books.

Schab, Lisa. 2008. *The Anxiety Workbook for Teens: Activities to Help You Deal with Anxiety and Worry.* Oakland, CA: New Harbinger Publications.

Resources for Anger

Lohmann, Raychelle. 2009. *The Anger Workbook for Teens: Activities to Help You Deal with Anger and Frustration.* Oakland, CA: New Harbinger Publications.

Resources for Self-Esteem and Assertiveness

Paterson, Randy J. 2000. *The Assertiveness Workbook: How to Express Your Ideas and Stand Up for Yourself at Work and in Relationships.* Oakland, CA: New Harbinger Publications.

Resources for Mindfulness

Brantley, Mary, and Tesilya Hanauer. 2008. *The Gift of Loving-Kindness: 100 Meditations on Compassion, Generosity, and Forgiveness.* Oakland, CA: New Harbinger Publications.

Germer, Christopher. 2009. *The Mindful Path to Self-Compassion: Freeing Yourself from Destructive Thoughts and Emotions.* New York: Guilford Press.

Johnson, Spencer. 1992. *The Precious Present.* Revised edition. New York: Doubleday.

Nhat Hanh, Thich. 1991. *Peace Is Every Step: The Path of Mindfulness in Everyday Life.* New York: Bantam Books.

Williams, Mark, John Teasdale, Zindel Segal, and Jon Kabat-Zinn. 2007. *The Mindful Way Through*

Depression: An 8-Week Program to Free Yourself from Depression and Emotional Distress. New York: Guilford Press.

Resources for Miscellaneous Topics

Brown, Brené. 2012. *Daring Greatly: How the Courage to Be Vulnerable Transforms the Way We Live, Love, Parent, and Lead.* New York: Gotham.

Shearin Karres, Erika. 2010. *Mean Chicks, Cliques, and Dirty Tricks: A Real Girl's Guide to Getting Though It All.* 2nd edition. Avon, MA: Adams Media.

Van Dijk, Sheri. 2015. *Relationship Skills 101 for Teens: Your Guide to Dealing with Daily Drama, Stress, and Difficult Emotions Using DBT.* Oakland, CA: New Harbinger Publications.

———. 2021. *The DBT Skills Workbook for Teen Self-Harm: Practical Tools to Help You Manage Emotions and Overcome Self-Harming Behaviors.* Oakland, CA: New Harbinger Publications.

References

Brantley, Mary, and Tesilya Hanauer. 2008. The Gift of Loving-Kindness: 100 Meditations on Compassion, Generosity, and Forgiveness. Oakland, CA: New Harbinger Publications.

Brown, Brené. 2012. Daring Greatly: How the Courage to Be Vulnerable Transforms the Way We Live, Love, Parent, and Lead. New York: Gotham Books.

Holt-Lunstad, Julianne, Timothy B. Smith, Mark Baker, Tyler Harris, and David Stephenson. 2015. "Loneliness and Social Isolation as Risk Factors for Mortality: A Meta-Analytic Review." Perspectives on Psychological Science 10 (2): 227–37.

Linehan, Marsha. 1993. Cognitive-Behavioral Treatment of Borderline Personality Disorder. New York: Guilford Press.

———. 2014. DBT Skills Training Manual. Second edition. New York: Guilford Press.

May, Gerald. 1982. Will and Spirit. New York: HarperCollins Publishers.

Van Dijk, Sheri. 2009. *The Dialectical Behavior Therapy Skills Workbook for Bipolar Disorder: Using DBT to Regain Control of Your Emotions and Your Life*. Oakland, CA: New Harbinger Publications.

_____. 2012. *Calming the Emotional Storm: Using Dialectical Behavior Therapy Skills to Manage Your Emotions and Balance Your Life*. Oakland, CA: New Harbinger Publications.

_____. 2021. *The DBT Skills Workbook for Teen Self-Harm: Practical Tools to Help You Manage Emotions and Overcome Self-Harming Behaviors*. Oakland, CA: New Harbinger Publications.

Sheri Van Dijk, MSW, is a psychotherapist and renowned dialectical behavior therapy (DBT) expert. She is author of several books, including *Don't Let Your Emotions Run Your Life for Teens* and *Calming the Emotional Storm*, and she presents extensively on this topic in Canada, the US, and abroad. Her books focus on using DBT skills to help people manage their emotions and cultivate lasting well-being. Van Dijk is recipient of the R.O. Jones Award from the Canadian Psychiatric Association.

More Instant Help Books for Teens
An Imprint of New Harbinger Publications

THE MINDFUL BREATHING WORKBOOK FOR TEENS
Simple Practices to Help You Manage Stress and Feel Better Now

THE STRESS REDUCTION CARD DECK FOR TEENS
52 Essential Mindfulness Skills

PUT YOUR FEELINGS HERE
A Creative DBT Journal for Teens with Intense Emotions

GOODNIGHT MIND FOR TEENS
Skills to Help You Quiet Noisy Thoughts and Get the Sleep You Need

CONQUER NEGATIVE THINKING FOR TEENS
A Workbook to Break the Nine Thought Habits That Are Holding You Back

THE DBT SKILLS WORKBOOK FOR TEEN SELF-HARM
Practical Tools to Help You Manage Emotions and Overcome Self-Harming Behaviors

newharbingerpublications
1-800-748-6273 / newharbinger.com

(VISA, MC, AMEX / prices subject to change without notice)
Follow Us

Don't miss out on new books in the subjects that interest you.
Sign up for our Book Alerts at **newharbinger.com/bookalerts**

Did you know there are free tools you can download for this book?

Free tools are things like **worksheets, guided meditation exercises**, and **more** that will help you get the most out of your book.

You can download free tools for this book—whether you bought or borrowed it, in any format, from any source—from the **New Harbinger** website. All you need is a NewHarbinger.com account. Just use the URL provided in this book to view the free tools that are available for it. Then, click on the "download" button for the free tool you want, and follow the prompts that appear to log in to your NewHarbinger.com account and download the material.

You can also save the free tools for this book to your **Free Tools Library** so you can access them again anytime, just by logging in to your account! Just look for this button on the book's free tools page:

+ save this to my free tools library

If you need help accessing or downloading free tools, visit **newharbinger.com/faq** or contact us at customerservice@newharbinger.com.

Back Cover Material

Take charge of your **emotions** & be your **best!**

Let's face it: life can give you plenty of reasons to feel frustrated, angry, sad, or even scared—and having those feelings is okay. But sometimes it can seem like your emotions are taking over, or spinning out of control with a mind of their own. To make matters worse, these overwhelming emotions might be interfering with school, causing trouble in your relationships, and preventing you from reaching your goals and enjoying your teen years.

A teen self-help classic, ***Don't Let Your Emotions Run Your Life for Teens*** has already helped thousands of teens just like you take charge of their emotions using proven-effective dialectical behavior therapy (DBT) skills. This fully revised and updated second edition provides even *more* strategies for dealing with difficult feelings, including new body-based practices for staying calm when intense emotions arise, and tips to help you focus on the things in life that make you feel happy and fulfilled.

This book offers powerful techniques to help you:

* Stay calmer and more mindful in times of stress
* Effectively manage out-of-control emotions

* Reduce the pain caused by your intense emotions
* Get along with family and friends

SHERI VAN DIJK, MSW, is a psychotherapist and renowned dialectical behavior therapy (DBT) expert. She is recipient of the R.O. Jones Award from the Canadian Psychiatric Association, and her work focuses on using DBT skills to help people manage emotions and cultivate well-being.

www.ingramcontent.com/pod-product-compliance
Lightning Source LLC
Chambersburg PA
CBHW011716220426
43662CB00018B/2400